Fresh Baked Manna

90 Days of Wisdom from the Word of God

Melva Henderson

Published by

Henderson House Publishing
4650 N. Port Washington Road
Glendale, WI 53212

ISBN: 978-0-9856573-0-7

Library of Congress Control Number: 2011906953

Contents

You're Covered in Prayer

Paul was known as an apostle, which means "a sent one," and had governing authority of several churches. He spent years laboring in the Word so the people in those churches would advance in their walk with Christ. One of the most powerful practices Paul engaged in was the practice of praying for the people in those churches. He literally poured his heart out before the Lord on behalf of the people, and those prayers are found in Ephesians 1:16–23, Ephesians 3:13–21, Philippians 1:9–11, and Colossians 1:9–14. They are known as the "Pauline Prayers."

As a minister, one of the greatest desires in my heart is to make sure I'm teaching the truth of God's Word in a way that people can receive it. I don't ever want to be found coming to my own conclusion about what God is saying, nor do I want to put things together in a way that is not useful to those receiving. The lives of people are too precious for ministers to play games or to neglect getting from God what is needed to feed them. A pastor is a shepherd, and Jesus is the greatest example of a pastor and apostle. The Bible calls Him "The Great Shepherd" because He feeds and cares for God's sheep in a way that no one else can.

Those of you who have decided to read *Fresh Baked Manna* are special people. You are deep in my heart, and every single day I'm seeking God for something relevant for your life. We may not know each other personally, but in my heart I'm connected to your life in some way. I think about you every day, just as I do my local church body, because I, like Paul, desire God's absolute best for you. It is amazing to me that it is possible to love and care for people that I don't even know.

What a minister gets to sense in cases like these is God's love for His people. It's actually God loving and reaching out to you through someone else. Yours is a life that God wants to touch and bless. He has ordained that our time in the Word should leave you full and enriched by His Spirit. That's a revelation and a mandate that I will never take lightly.

Every morning I lift you in prayer using the prayers that Paul prayed for the different churches, because they are God's desire for you. Here is just one of those prayers:

Father, I bow in prayer to you because of my work among the

1

Fresh Baked Manna *readers. Use your glorious riches to make every one of them strong. May your Holy Spirit reveal to them your power deep down inside. Then Christ will live firmly in their hearts because they believe in you. I pray that their love will have deep roots and a strong foundation. May they have power with all your people to understand Christ's love and know how wide, long, high, and deep that love is. Allow them to know your love, even though it can't be completely known, and then they will be filled with everything you have for them. God, you are able to do far more than they could ever ask for or imagine. Help them to do everything by your power that is working in them. I give you glory in the church, the lives of the readers of* Fresh Baked Manna *and in Christ Jesus, forever and ever. Amen!* (Ephesians 3:14–21 NIRV)

Just thought you'd like to know that you are covered in prayer and you are more than an acquaintance. This is a God-ordained partnership. God bless you today!!

Today's Scriptures: Ephesians 1:16–23; Ephesians 3:13–21; Philippians 1:9–11; Colossians 1:9–14.

Today's Prayer/Confession: Today I recognize that prayer is essential to my life. I will pray the Word and watch as God's plan unfolds for me.

Your Daily Devotion

Devotionals are meant to lead you to a place where your heart is directed toward the Father. They are written and designed to lead you into times of intimacy with Him. When you're done reading, if all you do is close the book and say, "That was good," you have missed the point. The word *devotional* comes from the root word *devotion,* which means "a profound dedication or consecration to something or someone." The word *devotional* is defined as "a short religious service." When you put these words together, your daily devotional should be a time when you participate in a short service dedicating and consecrating yourself to God.

Every day of your life God wants to enter into fellowship with you. He does not want you to have a "religious" experience, but rather a personal, life-changing encounter. The "busy-ness" of the day can drown out the voice of God, leaving you feeling empty and unsatisfied. However, there is a place of fulfillment that each of us can experience—a place where the cries and desires of our hearts are satisfied.

Most people have had what I like to call a "sweet conversion," a salvation experience marked as a time of pureness and intimacy with God. They prayed often and had a deep hunger for the Word of God, entering often into fellowship with the saints. Today, many have gotten away from the sweet communion of the Holy Ghost and live their lives independent of the presence of God. God didn't change. They did. But thank God that He's drawing us back to our place of hunger and personal intimacy with Him.

God is the one who places the desire for Himself within us, so we can't ignore the tug. When people don't understand this, they can be found seeking satisfaction in other people, places, or things. But they cannot satisfy the longings of the heart designed for only God to fill. If you find yourself so busy that there is no time for God, you are too busy. Make time and allow yourself the privilege of having a fellowship with Him.

Today I want to encourage you to take advantage of what God has provided for you through these daily devotionals. Have your own private service with Him. Let the Word of God feed your heart and draw you closer to the Father. He longs to have fellowship with you and you alone. Do yourself a favor and step back into your place of sweetness, draw on the love of the Father, and watch your love for Him grow deeper and stronger. Love to you all!

"And ye shall seek me, and find me, when ye shall search for me with all your heart" (Jeremiah 29:13).

Today's Scripture: Jeremiah 29:13.

Today's Prayer/Confession: Father, today I determine in my heart to seek you as I've never done before. I will keep my heart and my life before you in a manner that brings glory to your name. I long for a deeper and fuller walk, and I thank you that through the blood of Jesus, I will find you when I set my heart to seek you.

The Sufficiency of God's Grace

God's grace has been awesome in my life. It has consistently led and sustained me as I've walked the path ordered by God just for me. In the eighties, I heard Charles Capps give a definition of the word *grace*. He said, "Grace is God's willingness to use His power and His ability on your behalf, even though you don't deserve it." I have held on to that definition of grace all these years because it keeps me more conscious of God's ability than my own.

As believers, we need a very real "up close and personal" view of God's grace. In 2 Corinthians 12:9, the Lord told Paul, *"My grace is sufficient for thee."* With that statement, He said a mouthful. The word *sufficient* in the Greek language is *"Arkeo,"* which means "to be possessed of unfailing strength, to defend or ward off, to be enough." In so many words, Jesus was saying, "Paul, the power and ability that I have given to you is possessed with the kind of strength that is unfailing. It can defend you and ward off all manner of evil and opposition. My grace is more than enough to sustain you no matter what you may have to go through."

I really like the idea that the power and ability God has given to us is "possessed." Something possessed is overtaken by the control and influence of another. The grace of God that has been imparted to you and me is under complete influence and control of God's power and strength. It won't fail us!

As you venture out into your day, remember that just as God's grace was sufficient for Paul, that same grace is sufficient for you!

Today's Scripture: 2 Corinthians 12:9.

Today's Prayer/Confession: I recognize God's grace in my life, and I acknowledge that it is enough for me today!

A Thankful Heart is a "Faith-Full" Heart

Life has its triumphs and pains. People may surprise, disappoint, and perplex us, but in spite of it all, God's sustaining power always sees us through. We can sometimes live our lives too inundated by our own situations and forget that God is God. We find ourselves spending more time complaining than we do giving God thanks. The situation might be disheartening and times might be tough, but as believers, we have a responsibility to look to the Word of God and make our response based on what He has spoken.

1 Thessalonians 5:18 says: *"In everything give thanks: for this is the will of God in Christ Jesus concerning you."* Notice that this passage says *"in* everything," not *"for* everything." This is important to note because not everything that happens in our lives is worth giving thanks for. If I give God thanks for everything, the inclination is to think that even the bad things that come into my life are acceptable to God when they are not.

The Bible says in James 1:17 that *"Every good gift and every perfect gift is from above, and cometh down from the Father of lights, with whom is no variableness, neither shadow of turning."* Good gifts come down from the Father. The Father doesn't give bad gifts.

God wants us to learn to give Him thanks in whatever circumstance we find ourselves in. Why? Why would God want me to give Him thanks when I'm sick or when I'm broke? Can't He see that I'm struggling? Can't He feel my pain? The answer is "yes." He can see your struggle and He can feel your pain. And He intends to do something about it. If you can thank God when you are in places of need and lack, you reveal your confident trust in Him.

Thanking God in everything is an outward sign of your confident trust in God. He can be trusted to take care of you. Give thanks and His everlasting mercy will shine brightly for you!

Today's Scriptures: 1 Thessalonians 5:18; James 1:17.

Today's Prayer/Confession: Today, in everything, I will thank God for His goodness and His grace!!!

The Flesh:
A Way of Thinking That Opposes God

I officially gave my heart to the Lord in 1972 and can remember the excitement and emotions I felt the day I confessed Jesus as Lord of my life. I was ten years old and certain that everything in my life was going to change for the better. All my troubles would be over because I was now a Christian. Little did I know that after accepting Jesus Christ I would have to contend with two enemies for the rest of my Christian life—the devil and my flesh.

If we take an honest look at our lives, we can probably see that we have had to deal most often with our flesh. Many times we find ourselves blaming the devil for things that are really the works of our flesh. I once heard a story about the devil who was sitting on a church step crying when a man walked up to him and asked, "Mr. Devil, what's wrong? Why are you sitting out here on these steps crying?"

The devil replied, "Those people are in there blaming me for stuff I didn't even do."

The devil gets the blame for everything. I'm not saying that he is not the culprit behind most of our challenges. He's a real devil and he's a real enemy. But the truth of the matter is that most of the struggles and challenges we face are generally because of the weakness of our flesh, not the devil. We've given the devil too much credit.

Jesus said in Mark 14:38, "*Watch ye and pray, lest ye enter into temptation. The spirit truly is ready, but the flesh is weak.*" The flesh is the unregenerate part of the human nature. It is a carnal way of thinking that does not line up with the Word of God. Many people think the flesh is merely the physical body, but the flesh is also a way of thinking. It's a mindset that opposes God. This is why we are encouraged in Ephesians 4:23 to be "*renewed in the spirit of our minds,*" and again in Romans 12:2 to be "*transformed by the renewing of our minds.*" When we are renewed and transformed in the spirit of our minds, we won't respond to the dictates of our flesh. When we willingly choose to follow the truth of the Word of God, our minds are transformed and our flesh is denied the opportunity to act out. This is what is referred to in Galatians 5:23–24 as the crucifixion of the flesh. When you deny your flesh the right to govern your life, your carnal way of thinking dies, and your life blossoms in a powerful way in Christ.

Don't allow yourself to think in a way that opposes God. Make a determination to align your thinking with God's Word so you can experience a transformation that not even the devil can stop! Have a great day!

Today's Scriptures: Mark 14:38; Ephesians 4:23; Romans 12:2; Galatians 5:23–24.

Today's Prayer/Confession: My flesh does not control me. I am being transformed into the image of Christ as I feed daily on the Word of God.

See Yourself as God Does

I am amazed at the countless believers who seem to struggle to see themselves the way God sees them. Too many believe the lies and deceptions of the devil before they believe the truth of God's Word. Psalms 139:14 states that we have been *"fearfully and wonderfully made."* The word *fearfully* comes from a Greek word that means "honored and revered." The word *wonderfully* means "to be distinguished and set apart." In other words, God has made us honorable. We are distinguished and set apart for His purpose.

As children of God we cannot afford to look at or buy into the image the enemy has of us. He doesn't want you to see yourself as you really are, because when you do, Satan loses ground in your life. When you can see that you have been made in God's image and likeness and you begin to walk in what you see, it changes your life forever.

This is why the Word of God is so important in our lives. The Word of God is the mirror we look into in order to keep the true image of ourselves in our own eyes. *"And we all, who with unveiled faces contemplate the Lord's glory, are being transformed into his image with ever-increasing glory, which comes from the Lord, who is the Spirit"* (2 Corinthians 3:18 TNIV). It's nice when someone else is able to see the glory of God on you, but it's an entirely different thing when you can see it for yourself.

Jeremiah 29:11 states that God's thoughts concerning you are peaceful and loving, not of evil. His thoughts will bring you to His expected end. God believes the best about you. His thoughts are high. God wants you to see and think of yourself as He does. He believes the best about you. He thought so highly of you that He was willing to sacrifice His only begotten Son for you. He thought enough of you to place His Spirit within you, and no other creature on earth qualifies to carry the Spirit of the living God. That makes you pretty special!

So the next time you are tempted to think or act or speak negatively toward yourself, remember this: Your life is of great value to God! He loves you deeply and has made you His very own!!

Today's Scriptures: Psalms 139:14; 2 Corinthians 3:18; Jeremiah 29:11.

Today's Prayer/Confession: Today I will view myself through the eyes of God's Word. I will not look at the things that are seen because they are temporal, but I will look at the things that are eternal. I am greater than what I seem!

Living in the 100 Percent

I've often wondered what the world will be like when I go home to be with the Lord. I want to believe I have influenced lives in a positive way. When I think about my life on the earth, there is something inside that wants to make sure that what I'm doing is God-ordained and that it really counts. There are a lot of things we don't know for certain, but one thing we do know is all of us will one day leave this earth. We are only given twenty-four hours a day and we have to make every second count. So while we are here, we should live every day in what I like to call "the 100 percent."

I remember watching an episode of *The Oprah Winfrey Show* and evangelist Dr. Billy Graham was her special guest. Oprah asked Dr. Graham if there was anything that he would do differently after traveling the world and winning so many souls to Christ. Dr. Graham's response was, "I'd spend more time praying." I was blown away. Here was Billy Graham, one of the greatest evangelists the world has ever known, someone who has won numbers into the millions to Christ, longing for a deeper life of prayer. I took Dr. Graham's words to mean that through prayer he could live in the 100 percent.

I wept thinking about all the wasted moments of my life and how I had lived in the 50 percent instead of the 100 percent. I thought about the 50 percent days when I had worked with my family and the ministry as a "prayer-less, wordless wonder." I thought about all the decisions made and directives given without fully seeking the counsel of the Lord through His Word and prayer.

I determined that day that I wasn't going to miss any more opportunities to commune with my Father in prayer. I wasn't going to miss another day of feeding on His Word. And that's the day I stepped into what I call "the 100 percent." Living in the 100 percent isn't living a flawless life. It is simply living your best life each moment of your life and doing it through the Word of God. Living in the 100 percent is doing all you can to enjoy the life God has given you.

John 10:10 (Amplified) says this: "*The thief comes only in order to steal and kill and destroy. I came that they may have and enjoy life, and have it in abundance (to the full, till it overflows).*" Living in the 100 percent is living John 10:10. The whole world wants an overflowing, abundant life, but it isn't possible apart from Christ! When Jesus comes into our heart, He brings with Him eternal life (John 3:15–16), which is 100 percent life.

As a believer you have it. You're not waiting for it. You currently have eternal, abundant life flowing in your spirit right now. By reading, speaking, and acting on the Word of God, you bring that life into manifestation. So many Christians are waiting for life to "happen," not realizing that life is abiding in them. Living in the 100 percent is allowing the life that resides within to impact and affect the world around you.

As you start your day, allow yourself the joy of living in the 100 percent. It's not a flawless life, but it is a Spirit-governed life.

Today's Scriptures: John 10:10; John 3:15–16.

Today's Prayer/Confession: Today as I feed on God's Word, spending time in His presence, He will empower me to live in the 100 percent. Today I have abundance of joy, abundance of peace, abundance of health, abundance of provision. I'm living life to the full, until it overflows!

Living a Private Life, Publicly

Each morning before I even open my eyes there is usually a word or an impression on my heart. The word is so real and close it's as if the word or impression were placed over me, just waiting for me to rise. This morning was no different. The impression of the Lord was to ensure that my private life aligns with my public life. As believers who have the Holy Spirit of Christ living within us, we can find ourselves acting a certain way when others are watching, but doing things differently in private, and I'm not just talking about sin.

We all know the famous quote, "Don't be a public success and a private failure." Ephesians 6:6 (NASB) says it this way: *"Not by way of eye service, as men-pleasers, but as slaves of Christ."* As a public figure, if I'm not watchful, I can find myself instructing people to do things, but then struggle to do them myself. It's somewhat like the preacher who asks his congregation to commit to a time of fasting while he is at a restaurant plowing down steak and potatoes.

God wants us to put great effort into building our private lives with Him. I'm referring to daily feeding on the Word, praying, walking in love, living by faith, and yielding to the voice of the Holy Spirit. Who we are publicly will be an overflow of who we are privately. Your children and family shouldn't see a different you outside the home than they do inside the home.

I once heard a testimony given by a six-year-old girl named Melody whose parents fought constantly. Her father was mean and often yelled at her, her siblings, and their mother. However, when the family walked through the doors of their church, Melody noticed an immediate shift in both her father and mother. She often watched as they hugged and spoke kind words to those at the church. At the tender age of six, she could tell that this kind of behavior wasn't right.

Our families and children, along with the rest of the world, are waiting to see people who are real and consistent—those who really are who they say they are. Whether we like it or not, we are being watched. Paul calls us "living epistles." An epistle is a letter that is read to a body of people. What Paul meant is that people are reading your life, and it's important for you to be who God says you are, with or without others watching. Both privately and publicly, you should be a person of great character who operates with the highest morals and ethics at all times. You may make mistakes, but be quick to get it right, and don't let your mistakes make you.

Never forget that every great individual has had issues that could make or break them. The ones who made it are those who were willing to discipline and keep themselves in check at all times. Stay close to the Word of God, deal with yourself privately, and God promises to reward you openly (Matthew 6:4). Have a great day!

Today's Scriptures: Ephesians 6:6; Matthew 6:4.

Today's Prayer/Confession: My life is an epistle seen and read by others. I am committed to living a life that represents Christ to my family and the world around me.

Don't You Worry about a Thing

Not too long ago, I was preparing to travel and had been up late into the night taking care of some last-minute details. I went to bed knowing I would only get a few hours of sleep because my flight was scheduled to leave very early the next morning. When I awoke, I had an immediate feeling of panic, as I thought I had overslept. I jumped out of bed and ran to see what time it was, only to find it to be significantly earlier than I believed. Still shaken by the thought of oversleeping, my body struggled to go back to sleep because worry had taken my rest. My heart was beating fast, and I was sweating and nervous. Before I could do anything else, I had to calm down and gather myself, because I had just experienced an anxiety attack.

Throughout the Body of Christ, people live their daily lives stressed out and worried. Believers all over the world suffer with anxiety attacks. An anxiety attack by definition is a panic disorder. I like to define an anxiety attack as fear that manifests itself in the physical body because of a real or imagined thought, idea, or suggestion.

The Holy Spirit through the Apostle Paul instructs us in Philippians 4:6 (NKJV), *"Be anxious for nothing, but in everything by prayer and supplication, with thanksgiving, let your requests be made known to God."* I like the amplified version of this text: *"Do not fret or have any anxiety about anything, but in every circumstance and in everything, by prayer and petition (definite requests), with thanksgiving, continue to make your wants known to God."* God doesn't want us to live with anxiety. He has commanded us not to. When we are anxious, we are apt to move out of fear and emotions instead of faith or the guidance of the Holy Spirit.

Trust is a major ally in the fight against anxiety and worry. Trust is total confidence in God and His word. This is why we are to pray instead of worry. Prayer is the manifestation of trust, and trust is the manifestation of faith. When we choose to pray about our circumstances instead of worrying, we show God that our trust is in Him, and He moves on our behalf. When I choose to pray instead of worrying, I acknowledge His wisdom is greater than my own, and no matter what may be going on in my life, my confidence is in Him. The result is victory. This is called walking by faith.

When we choose to walk by faith, God replaces worry and anxiety with His peace and joy. When we choose to walk in fear, Satan replaces our joy and peace with his worry and anxiety. We have to be watchful because fear is perverted faith. It's faith in reverse. When you are anxious, you are still walking by faith; it's just perverted. You have more confidence in what the enemy can do to you than in what God can do for you.

When images of failure, loneliness, and confusion constantly bombard your mind, they bring fear and anxiety. However, a daily washing of the mind with the Word of God will remove these things from your life. For this reason, we must keep the Word of God before our eyes and in our ears. When we daily spend time feeding on God's Word, it increases our faith and fortifies our stand, keeping us grounded so the attacks of the enemy don't shake us.

You don't have to worry about a thing, because God has promised to be with you and take care of you. He promised He would never leave you nor forsake you. Hebrews 13:5–6 (Amplified) says:

> *Let your character or moral disposition be free from love of money [including greed, avarice, lust, and craving for earthly possessions] and be satisfied with your present [circumstances and with what you have]; for He [God] Himself has said, I will not in any way fail you nor give you up nor leave you without support. [I will] not, [I will] not, [I will] not in any degree leave you helpless nor forsake nor let [you] down (relax My hold on you)! [Assuredly not!] So we take comfort and are encouraged and confidently and boldly say, The Lord is my Helper; I will not be seized with alarm [I will not fear or dread or be terrified]. What can man do to me?*

Reinforce these truths in your mind and heart. Stay in the Word of God! If you struggle with worry and anxiety, let it stop today! God's Word is filled with peace, life and power! It not only has the ability to change your circumstances, but it will also change you!

"Trust in the Lord with all thine heart, and lean not unto thine own understanding. In all thy ways acknowledge him, and he shall direct thy paths" (Proverbs 3:5).

Today's Scriptures: Philippians 4:6; Hebrews 13:5–6; Proverbs 3:5.

Today's Prayer/Confession: I will trust in the Lord with all my heart. I will not lean to my own understanding, and in all my ways I will acknowledge Him today, and He will direct my path. I trust God!

Silence Really Is Golden

Have you ever been around someone who seemed to talk all the time? They just never appear to quiet themselves? When I was a little girl, I remember my grandmother telling me, "Lynn (my middle name), some people talk so much, it's like they have diarrhea of the mouth! You make sure that you keep your mouth closed!" Although this was humorous, I have never forgotten my grandmother's words. They have been with me all these years and helped form the foundation of who I am today. I have endeavored to be slow to speak and swift to hear, and although at times this may be frustrating to others, it has proven to be the wisdom of God for my life.

We have to spend more time training ourselves to listen, because when we don't, we run the risk of missing the voice of God. God, through the person of the Holy Spirit, is always speaking to us. His voice comes to lead and guide, but unfortunately we often miss His voice because all we can ever hear is our own. Psalms 29:4 says: *"The voice of the Lord is powerful,"* yet it comes to us in peace and stillness.

But the LORD was not in the wind: and after the wind an earthquake; but the Lord was not in the earthquake: And after the earthquake a fire; but the LORD was not in the fire: and after the fire a still small voice. (1 Kings 19:11–12)

There are two primary ways in which God speaks to us. The first is through His Word. Psalms 119:105 says: *"Thy word is a lamp unto my feet and a light unto my path."* Secondly, He speaks to us through our own human spirit. *"The spirit of man is the candle of the Lord, searching all the inward parts of the belly"* (Proverbs 20:27). Both require an acute ability to listen. God has so much that He wants to communicate to us, and fine-tuning our spiritual ears to His voice is vital. If you talk more than you listen, you will miss impartations, encouragement, and direction that you may need in the days to come.

One of my greatest frustrations in ministry is when I counsel someone who does all the talking. I'm often left thinking, "Why in the world did you call me if you have all the answers?" This is the way we can find ourselves operating with God. He knows everything and has all the answers, and yet when we come to Him, we do all the talking. Psalms

46:10 says: *"Be still and know that I am God."* I like to say it like this: "Be quiet, and let God be God!"

The Lord spoke to me today and said, "Your ability to hear my voice is only as great as your ability to close your mouth." We don't want to find ourselves in the presence of the God of the whole universe (the one who created heaven and earth) and realize we are doing all the talking. He has something to say! I once heard a man of God say, "One word from God can change your life forever." If just one word can change our lives, imagine what an entire sentence will do if we take the time to listen and receive what He has to say.

As you venture out to begin your day, be purposeful about listening to the voice of the Lord. Spend time meditating on the Word of God, and then focus on your spirit. You'll be amazed at what the Lord has to say.

Today's Scriptures: Psalms 29:4; 1 Kings 19:11–12; Psalms 119:105; Proverbs 20:27; Psalms 46:10.

Today's Prayer/Confession: Today I set myself to hear the voice of the Lord. I will quiet myself to hear what He has to say to my heart.

Whom the Lord Loves, He Corrects

We are all usually happy about the goodness of God. When we acknowledge Him as our Father, it should prompt us to praise and worship Him for all that He has done for us. There's not one day that should go by that we don't recognize how wonderful and good He has been toward us. But what about those days He has to correct us or expose something in our lives that isn't good for us or pleasing to Him? How wonderful is He to you then? Can you still appreciate Him when He reveals or exposes wrong motives or intentions in your life?

God spoke to my heart one day and very specifically stated that I was off focus in a particular place in my home life. There were adjustments that needed to be made in order for me to grow in this area. Although I didn't particularly like it, I had to make these adjustments and submit to what God had revealed. Whether we realize it or not, God cares about our lives. If we allow Him to, He will get involved in areas we wouldn't imagine He would be interested in.

Proverbs 3:5 says, *"Trust in the Lord with all thine heart, and lean not unto thine own understanding. In all thy ways acknowledge him and he shall direct thy paths."* I used to think this scripture meant acknowledge Him in spiritual matters, but the text says in all my ways I am to acknowledge Him, which leaves nothing out. If I'm taking care of my kids, that's one of my ways. If I'm going to the grocery store, that's one of my ways. It doesn't matter what I do or where I go, all of my ways are of interest to God.

When we accepted Christ, we didn't just get saved from hell. We were also afforded the opportunity and privilege of engaging in a personal relationship with God, and He gets involved. When I embraced God as my heavenly Father, I submitted my entire life to Him. If my ways on any given day fail to line up with His character or His Word, because we are in a relationship, He has the right and responsibility to correct me.

Because I am a married woman, my husband has the right to get involved in the day-to-day affairs of my life. There is no area that is off limits to him, and the same goes for my right to get involved in his life. We understand that we chose to be in this marriage relationship, and the idea of personal privacy is a thing of the past. I forfeited the option of shutting out his input and correction as it relates to my life when I entered into the marriage covenant. The same is true with God. As His children, we have entered into a covenant, and He has the absolute right to correct us whenever we need it. Proverbs 3:12 states that the Lord loves those He corrects. The implication is if you are not corrected by the Lord, then you are not loved by Him. I once heard someone say, "God accepts me just the way I am, but He loves me too much to let me stay this way."

I remember dating a man prior to marriage who I thought could possibly have been "the one." This individual put on a really good show. He knew all the Christian jargon and attended church regularly. I quickly found out, however, that his life was full of sin and he had never fully committed his heart to Christ. The Lord sent a friend I considered an accountability partner to me and she said, "Melva, he's not the one. This is not God's selection for you." I remember being extremely angry, not just at my friend, but at God. In my flesh, I really liked this man, and even though I could see visible signs that should have raised my spiritual antennas, I ignored them because of his so-called "spiritual depth" and his physical "fineness." I thought he was the man God had chosen for me, but I was wrong

My friend's words sent me into a time of prayer and fasting, and I heard myself crying out to God, "Why don't you want me happy? Why does it seem like everybody else can make decisions about their lives and you bless them, but when I make decisions, you always trump them?" My words were extreme but that's how I felt at that time. I will never forget what God said to me as I sat and listened for His response. His words came to me: "It's because of your prayers, Melva. You asked me as a twelve-year-old girl not to allow anything in your life that didn't please me. You asked me to keep you and protect you. All I am doing is honoring what you have requested of me." That was over twenty years ago, but it still touches my heart as if He said it to me today.

What if He had not corrected me? What if I had married the man anyway? I'm so glad He corrected me, and because I obeyed, He sent a precious, powerful man into my life. He wasn't as savvy as the other gentleman, and at that time he wasn't a mature believer, but his heart was right. Today God is using him to forcefully advance His Kingdom.

Today, as you listen to the voice of the Holy Spirit, be open to what He speaks to you and obey Him. Let Him love you and bring correction to your life. Remember, He only corrects those He loves.

God bless you and may increase come to you today!

Today's Scriptures: Proverbs 3:5; Proverbs 3:12.

Today's Prayer/Confession: As a child of God, I will respond to the voice of the Lord. I will obey His direction for my life.

Prosperity and Pleasure Come through Discipline

One of the most difficult battles in life is the battle of self-discipline. Discipline alone is a word that our flesh (mine included) would love to rip out of the English language in its entirety. Unfortunately, we don't have this as an option, and even if we did, we would still have to contend with discipline, because it's implied numerous times throughout the Bible. If we were to mention the word in most circles, it would trigger various thoughts, but a resounding one would be that discipline can be very difficult.

Discipline is defined as "training to act in accordance with rules; punishment inflicted by way of correction and training." I like to define it like this: "Discipline is your ability to maintain and apply pressure on your behavior on a daily basis in order to improve or develop yourself."

Discipline is not an easy thing. It takes time, effort, and a denial of self that most are not willing to endure. It's something you must do for yourself on purpose. No one can discipline you but you. God can't, and neither can your pastor, spouse, therapist, small group leader, or friend. You are the only individual who can discipline you. That's why it's called "self-discipline."

I would love to lie down and leave the responsibility for change in my life with God. It's easier that way. Then I don't have to take responsibility for my own actions or my own ways. It would always be God's fault or someone else's fault that I keep having the struggles I do in life. It's like those monkeys you see cleaning each other off. One is lying down while the other is doing all the work. The one lying down has no interest in cleaning himself. He is just basking in the sun, enjoying the work of someone else. If he's not clean behind the ears, it's not his fault, because he didn't give himself the bath.

That's not the way it is with us. Your transformation in life comes from placing your own foot in God's spiritual bathtub and applying the water and soap of the Word of God to your own life. Your weight loss will come when you tell yourself "that's enough" and put daily pressure on yourself to live by the standards you have set, even though it's hard. Your addictive behaviors will change when you feed on the Word of God, change the way you think, and then act on that change, even though it's hard. Again, you have to do it! There are situations where we will need someone to walk with us, but they are walking *with* us, not walking *for* us.

One day, my oldest daughter wasn't feeling well and needed to get to her bed. She is almost thirty years old and weighs 110 pounds: I am only one pound lighter than she is. I could not physically lift her, but I was determined to get her to the bed. I mustered all the strength I had to help her, but when it was time to walk, my daughter had to make herself take the steps toward the bed. Yes, I helped her. I walked with her every step of the way. I became a weight bearer, but I could not walk or get into the bed for her. Had I walked for her, she would never have made it to the bed.

You have to recognize that you have been given the tools to live an overcoming life. You have to use those tools on yourself. You simply cannot allow yourself to act or think whatever or however you want, expecting someone else to come along and make the change. No, sir! No, ma'am! It's all on you. God requires that we learn to put pressure on ourselves so we can walk in the fullness of what He has provided for us.

Job's friend, Elihu, made an important statement about God: *"He openeth also their ear to discipline, and commandeth that they return from iniquity. If they obey and serve him, they shall spend their days in prosperity, and their years in pleasures."* (Job 36:10–11).

Prosperity and having years of pleasure are the rewards of living a disciplined life. As you begin your day, determine to exercise self-control and discipline. Listen to the voice of your spirit, and stop when you hear "That's enough!" You'll begin to see prosperity and experience true pleasure as never before.

God bless you and have a disciplined day!

Today's Scripture: Job 36:10–11.

Today's Prayer/Confession: Today I will discipline myself. I will obey and serve God, and I will walk in prosperity and experience Godly pleasures.

The Lord of the Breakthrough

And the Philistines came and spread themselves in the valley of Rephaim. And David enquired of God, saying, Shall I go up against the Philistines? And wilt thou deliver them into mine hand? And the LORD said unto him, Go up; for I will deliver them into thine hand. So they came up to Baalperazim; and David smote them there. Then David said, God hath broken in upon mine enemies by mine hand like the breaking forth of waters: therefore they called the name of that place Baalperazim. (1 Chronicles 14:8–11)

In the above passage, God gave David and his men victory over the Philistines. After David won the battle, he called the place *Baalperazim*, which means "Lord of the Breakthrough."

Before you and I were born again, Satan did all he could to stop us from accepting and moving forward in Christ. It's kind of like the Looney Tunes character Wile E. Coyote, who works overtime endeavoring to stop the Road Runner. Satan doesn't want us to receive Jesus into our hearts, but because he realizes he can't stop us, he continually attempts to keep us ignorant of who we are and what we have in Christ. He continually works by building walls of ignorance, or as someone once called them "walls of containment."

A wall of containment won't let anything in or out. It's a wall that keeps you in the same place experiencing the same thing all the time. It will allow you to have your needs met, but that's it. You can't go beyond just having your needs met, because the wall of containment blocks the floods of overflow and abundance, keeping you living with just enough. But the scripture reveals God as *El Shaddai*, the God of more than enough (Exodus 6:3).

When we find ourselves satisfied with the same ol' same ol', not wanting more or going after anything greater, it's likely that we have Satan's walls of containment around us. But God wants us to break out of those walls and walk in the fullness of all He has provided for us. Remember, He is *Baalperazim*, the "Lord of the Breakthrough." This is a truth many of us need in our lives today. God has promised and made available so much for us, but for some reason we fail to walk in the reality of what He has provided.

It's time to wake up and recognize that we have a responsibility to walk in all that God has given us. Walking in the fullness of God's blessing is a requirement for a believer, because God wants the people and nations of this earth to see that He is with His people and that He has blessed them. This is not just in the area of finances. This is also in the areas of peace, health, and relationships. It encompasses every area of our lives, both spiritual and natural.

Let the Lord of the Breakthrough knock down every wall in your life. Leave no stone standing, because every stone erected represents a place of containment. God has great things in store for you. He wants to increase you and fill you to overflowing. Let Him do it. You'll be so glad you did!

Today's Scriptures: 1 Chronicles 14:8–11; Exodus 6:3.

Today's Prayer/Confession: Lord, I declare that any wall of containment in my life is coming down today, in Jesus's name! I will walk in the fullness of the blessing of God, and nothing will hinder me or hold me back.

Grace for Today

When I was a student in Bible School, one of my teachers made this statement: "When your output exceeds your input, then your upkeep will be your downfall." At that time, I couldn't relate to it. But then I had an overwhelming experience while taking care of my husband, working in ministry, juggling my children, cleaning my house, grocery shopping, helping others, and dealing with many other responsibilities.

All of us may experience days of feeling overwhelmed, but being overwhelmed comes from putting out more than we take in. God gives us grace sufficient for today. We don't get grace for tomorrow until tomorrow. Jesus said in Matthew 6:34 that tomorrow would take care of itself. The mercies God extends to us are new for today. The grace and ability to do all we must do is for our lives today. Don't let thoughts about tomorrow overwhelm you. Live your best life today. A lot of frustrated people are trying to squeeze a week's or a month's worth of work into a single day, and this results in a continual pouring out. We end up doing double duty, trying to accomplish today's responsibilities and those of the future. We find ourselves in a perpetual place of giving, and there is no time to receive.

God wants to fill our lives with all that is necessary to accomplish our day-to-day tasks and responsibilities. The key to ensuring a peaceful and accomplished day is sitting in the presence of God, feeding on His Word, and allowing Him to fill us with all we need for the day. God knows we have the responsibilities we do. In fact, He has promised to direct our ways if we acknowledge Him (Proverbs 3:6). He will give us wisdom and understanding in a way that will allow us to complete our tasks in record time. When we put Him first, everything lines up. There is no toil, no stress, and no emotional or physical breakdown, because we are following God's order for our day. He is a Father who knows we have responsibilities on the earth. He's not selfish. He just wants to be in our lives so we can live our natural lives supernaturally.

If you've been experiencing thoughts of quitting, leaving, or even "checking out," it may be that you just need to spend some time receiving. Sit down and quiet yourself. Let the Lord speak to you. Take a deep breath and allow the Holy Spirit to fill your atmosphere with His love and presence. When you are full, you can then take on the many duties of the day. Let Him in. He longs to help you!

Today's Scriptures: Matthew 6:34; Proverbs 3:6.

Today's Prayer/Confession: Today I have the grace necessary to accomplish all that God sets before me. I will not stress. I will not toil. I will walk in the grace and ability of God and all will be well with me.

The Freedom of an Open Heart

Sometimes we can find ourselves moving along to the sound of a certain beat. It's not a bad beat and it's not a good beat—it's just a beat. We get so used to hearing a daily "move it along" that we can become mechanical, almost robotic, in our lives. This is especially true as Christians. We say "Amen" and "Hallelujah" in all the right places, but our heart is somewhere else. We have to watch our hearts to make sure what comes out of them is always real and pure toward God.

When we approach God, we should always come with the intent to pour out the abundance of our heart, releasing whatever is sitting at the top and working our way to its depth. When this is done, we can get to the core of matters, and once the heart has been relieved, it brings a soothing to the soul.

There was a time when I struggled to open up my heart to God. I was mechanical and religious instead of open and honest. I heard the Holy Spirit gently say, "If you pray from a truthful, honest place, a place of openness, I will speak to you." I immediately stopped "moving to the beat" and quieted myself. I connected my tongue with my heart and began effectively pouring out to God all I had been carrying.

But nothing happened until I prayed from a truthful and open place. God knows and sees what's going on, and His attention is on our hearts. King David understood this principle of keeping your heart pure before God. In Psalms 51:6 he said, *"Behold, thou desirest truth in the inward parts: and in the hidden part thou shalt make me to know wisdom."* The New Living Translation puts it this way: *"But you desire honesty from the heart, so you can teach me to be wise in my inmost being."* That's really good!

God wants a heart He can use. He wants a heart that will seek Him with nothing hidden. Psalms 66:18 states: *"If I regard iniquity in my heart, the Lord will not hear me."* No matter what you may have done or how you may feel, approach God from a pure place and He will, as Psalms 51:6 says, cause you to know wisdom.

Today as you talk with the Lord, speak to Him from a pure open place and listen as He guides and directs you into places of honor and truth. Have an awesome day!

Today's Scriptures: Psalms 51:6; Psalms 66:18.

Today's Prayer/Confession: Lord, today I will open my heart to you. I will engage openly and honestly with you, and I won't hold anything back.

Rise and Be Healed

This morning a song rang in my heart. "Rise and be healed in the name of Jesus; let your faith arise in your soul. Rise and be healed in the name of Jesus; He will cleanse you and make you whole." As I pondered these words, I realized that I was being commanded by the Holy Spirit to "rise and be healed in the name of Jesus." Every time I thought about it, it touched my heart and gave me the strength I needed for today. Healing isn't just for the aches, pains, and diseases we experience in the physical body. Healing is also for the aches, pains, and "dis-eases" we experience in our hearts.

As a Christian, you have to make yourself remember that you are not greater than your Lord. Our Lord Jesus experienced hurtful, heart-wrenching things by the hands and words of men. These things could have cut Him to the core. He was disrespected, mistreated, lied about and abandoned. Even worse is the fact that He was misunderstood and denied by those closest to Him, those He helped the most. If men disappointed Him, don't be surprised if they disappoint you.

There is a very interesting statement in John 2:24 (NIV): *"But Jesus would not entrust himself to them, for he knew all men."* The Message Bible says it like this: *"But Jesus didn't entrust his life to them. He knew them inside and out, knew how untrustworthy they were."* If we could learn this truth, we would avoid a great deal of heartache. God wants us to entrust our lives to Him and Him alone. The carnal nature of man cannot be trusted because it's inconsistent. It loves you today and will hate or despise you tomorrow if it doesn't get its way.

While Jesus was hanging on the cross, He looked down at His persecutors and prayed, "Father, forgive them for they know not what they do." I find that most individuals don't really realize what they are doing. Even though their hearts may be wrong, in some cases they really can't see how damaging their words or actions are toward another brother or sister. They cannot see that they are possibly being used by the devil. So we have to be like Jesus and pray for them. Matthew 5:44 (Message) says this: *"I'm telling you to love your enemies. Let them bring out the best in you, not the worst. When someone gives you a hard time, respond with the energies of prayer."*

It's interesting to note that just as they couldn't see the negative impact of their actions, they also couldn't see the positive impact. When Jesus was being crucified, it was the most horrific experience that anyone had ever or will ever go through. Satan clearly thought he had unleashed his best. But when it was over, Jesus was the glorified and reigning Lord of all. The worst curse actually gave way to the greatest blessing! In fact, 1 Corinthians 2:8 says that if Satan had known that his persecution was going to backfire, he never would have crucified Jesus, the Lord of Glory! That makes me want to laugh! Satan couldn't see how his attack was going to bless the whole world, and he can't see how using other people to come against you will bless your world. But it will. To use modern-day terminology, all your "haters" are positioning you for a manifestation of the glory of God!

Let their attack bring out the best in you. Keep your heart right. Let the love of God step forward. Keep a clear understanding of who you are, what's going on, and how it's going to turn out. Don't let words or actions break you. Stand firm knowing you are more than a conqueror and no weapon formed against you will ever prosper, even if they think it will. God's got you, and when it's all said and done, you will be the one standing with the glory of God all around you. Rise and be healed in the name of Jesus!

Today's Scriptures: John 2:24; Matthew 5:44; 1 Corinthians 2:8.

Today's Prayer/Confession: I choose to forgive those who come against me. I release the love of God and believe the absolute best for them!

Wisdom for the Day

There are thirty-one days in most months and there are thirty-one Proverbs in the Bible. Since I was a young believer, I have read one Proverb every morning because it is filled with wisdom and knowledge that builds and shapes the character. Some mornings a specific word or passage will really minister to me. It almost "stands up" off the page, and there is a gentle pull on my heart to read it over and over again. I've found myself reading a scripture as many as twenty to thirty times, and then I'll walk away meditating on it (repeating it to myself, either out loud or under my breath) while I'm preparing my home and family for the day. What am I doing? I'm hiding and planting the Word in my heart, and the Word I'm hiding automatically begins the process of transformation (Romans 12:1–2).

Many want to walk with God, but they fail to realize that walking with God is more than just being a Christian. It is establishing a life in the Word, maintaining your love walk, and cultivating a solid position in prayer. To walk with God is to walk with His Word. We simply cannot know God apart from His Word. We can have a limited understanding of Him because we experience His love, mercy, and grace, but to really "know" Him, to come into places of intimacy with Him, we have to seek Him out through His Word.

The Word reveals who God is, how He acts, and what His character is like. As in any relationship, spending time together is essential for its security and longevity. We don't want to find ourselves merely acknowledging God as our Father but living void of the reality of the relationship. When we look at our lives, we should see God in operation and in manifestation in every area. When we spend time feeding on the Word of God, we are able to recognize all that we are, all that we have, and all that we can do because of the power of Christ residing and working in us. With God we can really "do all things through Christ which strengthens us," but if we don't draw wisdom out of the Word of God, we will act as if it doesn't exist, and live that day without it.

As you begin your day interacting with family, co-workers, and friends, don't forget the most important interaction—time with the wisdom of

God, which is time in the Word of God. Let the Word speak to you today, and receive the wisdom and understanding you need. God bless!

Today's Scripture: Romans 12:1–2.

Today's Prayer/Confession: Lord, today I will feed on your Word. And as I do, I will walk in your wisdom and be of quick understanding.

Without His Grace

Where would I be
You only know
So glad you see
Through eyes of love
A hopeless case
An empty place
Without your grace...

These are the words of a song and they flow deep in my heart. Sometimes it's good to think back and reflect on the love and grace of God. Ephesians 2:12 tells us to remember where the Lord has brought us from, not dwelling on the sins of our past, but comparing and contrasting our lives before we walked with God to our lives after we accepted Christ as Lord and Savior. He wants us to recall the fact that we were in sin, without hope, and apart from Him. But His power redeemed, blessed, and raised us to newness of life!

Remember that at that time you were separate from Christ, excluded from citizenship in Israel and foreigners to the covenants of the promise, without hope and without God in the world (Ephesians 2:12 NIV).

I can honestly say I don't know what my life would be like without Jesus. When I look in the eyes of some of the people in the world, and even in the church my heart aches. I can see they are devoid of life, when in reality, they don't have to be. David said in Psalms 23, "The Lord is our shepherd." He went on to say, "He prepares a table before us in the presence of our enemy." God has made available to every one of us a table spread out with His blessings. On that table, we will find the blessing of healing and health, the blessing of financial provision and prosperity, the blessing of deliverance from bondage and hang-ups, and the blessing of restored family relationships. These are just a few of the blessings we can expect.

If you look at your life today and you can still see "a hopeless case" or an "empty place," you need another vision. Open the Word of God and take advantage of His grace. It's available to you right now. If you can't see the manifestation of the blessing of God in operation in your life, just think of where He brought you from. All God has is yours. It's there for the taking. Jesus wants the empty places in your life filled, and He wants to replace hopelessness with hope. Let Him do it today!

Where would you be if not for His grace?

Today's Scriptures: Ephesians 2:2–14; Psalms 23.

Today's Prayer/Confession: Today as I look back over my life, I give God praise for all He has done for me. Lord, thank you for your grace!

Are You Living?

Consider this: Jesus said in John 10:10 (Amplified), *"The thief comes only in order to steal and kill and destroy. I came that they may have and enjoy LIFE, and have it in abundance, to the full, until it over flows."*

The word *life* comes from the Greek word *Zoe*, which is "the absolute fullness of life, real and genuine, a life active and vigorous, devoted to God, blessed, endless life."

Zoe is eternal life. It's the God kind, or God quality of life. When we were born again, Zoe was imparted into our spirits. The inward power of Zoe produces the outward ability to live a victorious, overflowing life. Do you believe this is God's will for you? Do you believe that you are supposed to have an overflowing, abundant life? Are you experiencing the God kind of life? If not, God wants your life to abound with blessings, both spiritual and natural. He wants your life to have *life*! If you were to take a self-inventory, would you say you are really living, or do you just exist? Are you living with just enough when God said in Genesis 17:1 that He is *"El Shaddai,"* the God who is more than enough?

The two most essential elements for living the God quality of life are the Word of God and your faith. The Word is our sustenance, our bread for life. Faith is the vehicle that helps us receive that life. By faith we access all God has promised. In order to keep the life of God in manifestation, you will have to commit yourself to feeding on God's Word and constantly releasing your faith. In the end, the Zoe inside of you will transform you into all God wants you to be.

God bless you and have a wonderful day!

Today's Scriptures: John 10:10; Genesis 17:1.

Today's Prayer/Confession: I have the life of God in me. I have His life, His nature, and His ability. I have the life of God in me!

Keep It Real!

This was another morning that the Word of the Lord seemed to hover over my head, and this is what was said: "Don't play games with me. Keep your heart open before me and I will change your life."

In our approach to God—whether it be times in the Word, times in prayer, or times attending church—if not watchful, we can find ourselves acting in a "religious" way. We don't want to do things out of habit or tradition, but rather from an overflowing of the heart. It is vital for us to approach God with the sincerest heart, knowing He can see what's going on within us anyway. He knows what's real.

As a young believer, I so deeply wanted to be spiritual. The problem was that I kept my eyes on people, and as a result, I grew in sensitivity to what they thought or expected of me, instead of growing in a true and genuine sensitivity to the Holy Spirit. I was becoming religious, not spiritual. My outward expressions toward God were manufactured. I knew the lingo and the jargon. I knew when and how to say it. I was developed enough to cry on cue. I was so busy "working" to have an experience with God that I missed precious opportunities for my heart to release itself before Him. Consequently, I lived an inwardly frustrated life and many times found myself with a deep sense of emptiness.

God can see the deepest intentions of your heart. He can see all of your "stuff," yet He longs for something real with you. As a pastor, over the years I have had the opportunity to look into the eyes of hundreds of individuals who struggle to believe they can be real with God and still be loved by Him. So they live with the fear of exposure. They think God is like man, but He's not. He accepts you as you are and pours out His love and grace in your life. God wants you to keep your heart in a place where He can do the work in you that must be done. But you can't hide. You can't resort to the fearful acts of masking, covering up, or acting like you think you should. God sees your heart, so give Him access to it.

The day you learn to live openly before God will be the day you begin to experience real, true freedom from pretense and fear. Fear will be a thing of the past, because your heart will be open to trust God.

As you start your day, determine not to be like the religious people in the days of Jesus who had a form of godliness but denied God's power.

The power of God was present to heal, deliver and to set them free, but they couldn't take advantage of it because they were stuck in their religious ways. They gave more credence to looking than to being right. Don't let that be your case. You have access to all that God is. Do not waste time acting or masking. "Let it all hang out" before Him, and you will see a manifestation of God's goodness and the joy of liberty as you never have before.

Today's Scriptures: 2 Timothy 3:5; Luke 5; Matthew 15:8.

Today's Prayer/Confession: Today I open my heart completely to God. I will not hold any part of who I am from Him, and I will walk free from religious bondages and fear.

Hold That Thought!

Lately I've been hearing this phraseology: "Sin will take you further than you want to go, keep you longer than you want to stay, and cost you more than you want to pay." Believe it or not, the same is true of your thoughts. If allowed, your thoughts will take you further than you need to go, keep you longer than you need to stay, and when acted on, will cost you more than you really want to pay.

There are many enemies we have in life. If I were to take a poll and ask people who they thought their enemies were, I can guarantee you the majority of those mentioned would fall under two categories—the devil and other people. But one enemy people often miss is the enemy "within-a-*me*"—the enemy of our own minds. Of all the wars the world has ever known, no war has been in existence as long as the war of the mind.

In order for us to grow as believers, we must learn the importance of controlling our thoughts. We can't be "cerebral renegades." Our thought life is very powerful. It has the potential to move us into success or drive us to absolute failure. Think about this: Because of thoughts people won't accept Christ, because of thoughts families have been destroyed, because of thoughts relationships have ended. If your thoughts don't line up with the Word of God, it is going to be difficult to advance in life. God wants you to have total life prosperity. This is not just money in the bank, but it is also peace in your mind. *"Beloved I wish above all things that thou mayest prosper and be in health, even as thy soul prospereth"* (3 John 1:2). The soul includes your thinking processes.

Early in our marriage, when my husband and I had a disagreement, he would always want to "deal with it later." I, on the other hand, needed to talk it out. After many years of marriage, I know better, but back then, "deal with it later" meant he wouldn't address the issue at all. I didn't want to "put him on the corner of the roof" (Proverbs 25:24), so even though I was frustrated, I would leave him alone. Unfortunately, the problem escalated, because even though I was not able to express it, I was having a full-blown confrontation with him in my mind.

Because I was left with my own thoughts, my mind took me further than I needed to go, and once I got out there, the devil was there to pedal thoughts even stronger than my own. "He doesn't love you," or, "He didn't care that you were left to deal with this alone." I was feeding on my thoughts and before I knew it, I was in his face holding a cast iron skillet, ready to let him have it. It's comical now, but back then it wasn't. We were arguing over who should have killed a centipede crawling on the kitchen wall. That was a light example of going further than we should have gone, but for some of us, the examples are far more extreme.

Casting down imaginations, and every high thing that exalteth itself against the knowledge of God, and bringing into captivity every thought to the obedience of Christ (2 Corinthians 10:5).

God wants you to deal with your thoughts, not just let them sit in your head. If they are ungodly, they have to be cast down. If not, you'll end up going where you didn't want to go. *Casting down* in Greek means "to throw down with force," like a king that has been dethroned, or a wrestler that is violently slammed to the ground by his opponent. The Word of God is the muscle that you use to bring your thoughts into obedience to Christ. By using the Word of God, you replace your thoughts with God's thoughts. Instead of thinking the worst, the Word will help you think the best.

Let the Word of God work in your life. Whenever you find yourself in the middle of a mental battle, wait for the Word to rise up from your heart. It's on the way. Joyce Meyer says: "You've got another think coming." So wait for it. Don't act on the negative. The positive always comes if you give place to the Word of God in your life.

Finally, brethren, whatsoever things are true, whatsoever things are honest, whatsoever things are just, whatsoever things are pure, whatsoever things are lovely, whatsoever things are of good report; if there be any virtue, and if there be any praise, think on these things (Philippians 4:8).

Today you are going to have marvelous opportunities for your mind to "take off," but put the weight of the Word of God on it and you'll be all right!

Today's Scriptures: 3 John 1:2; Proverbs 25:24; 2 Corinthians 10:5; Philippians 4:8.

Today's Prayer/Confession: Today I will align my thoughts with the Word of God and cast down every thought that doesn't line up with God's Word.

Days of Heaven on Earth

Eternity is a word that most people don't like to think about and something many won't even talk about. But whether we like it or not, every one of us will one day leave this earth. Now some of you might not want to read the rest of this because of what I just said, but hang on, because it's going to get better.

As a child I remember the saints of old talking and singing about heaven. They would clap their hands, pat their feet, and look up in the sky. It almost seemed as though their faces would light up, glowing with the thought of being with Jesus and walking the streets "paved with gold." I, on the other hand, would stand mortified at the very idea that I would one day have to die to walk the streets "paved with gold." Don't get me wrong, I wanted to see heaven. I just didn't want to have to die to see it. It's amazing that although I know going to heaven is inevitable for me, there still remains something deep within that doesn't want to have to die to see it. I once heard a man say, "Everybody is talking about the sweet by and by, but what about the rotten here and now?" I concur!

When God created the Garden of Eden, He placed within it everything man would need to live a lavish life. The Garden of Eden was a place of abundance. It was full of provision. It overflowed with the blessing of the Lord, and it was created solely for mankind. This was God's revealed will for man at creation, and if He wanted abundant living for us then, He wants it for us now. God does not change. God wants you to have days of heaven on the earth (Deuteronomy 11:21). He wants you to have more than enough in your life here on earth. God's provision has a three-fold purpose: 1) to bless you; 2) to advance His Kingdom; and 3) to bless others. But you can't be a blessing to others if you're not blessed yourself.

It is difficult to be a student of the Word of God and not see God's provision throughout. People struggle in life, hoping and praying that one day their "ship will come in." Well I'm here to tell you that the ship isn't coming in. It's already in! It came in when Jesus gave us access to the blessing that God invoked upon Abraham (Galatians 3). Your ship is in, and though you may not be able to see it in the natural, if you are a believer, it's there in the spirit and it's yours for the taking.

Everything we receive from God we do by an act of our faith. When we learn what is rightfully ours, based on the Word of God, we can pull it out of the supernatural realm into the natural realm, but it's done by faith.

While we look not at the things which are seen, but at the things which are not seen: for the things which are seen are temporal; but the things which are not seen are eternal (2 Corinthians 4:18).

There is another realm of existence that we have access to. It is called the realm of the Spirit. How do we look at things not visible if they don't exist? They have to exist in order for us to look at them, but we can only see them with the eye of faith. Everything, no matter what it is, started out in the unseen realm first. If you can't see your provision with your spiritual eye, you will never see it with the natural eye, because again, everything starts out in the unseen before it is seen. We have to understand this truth in order to be able to see that God has already provided for us.

Don't wait until you die to live the abundant life. Recognize that there is another place of provision for you, and if the brooks in your life have dried up, know that God has a flowing stream of blessings for you that will *never* dry up. Ask God to open your eyes and appropriate all He has provided for you. God bless you and let today be a day of heaven on earth!

Today's Scriptures: Deuteronomy 11:21; Galatians 3; 2 Corinthians 4:18.

Today's Prayer/Confession: Father, open the eyes of my spirit so I can see all that you have provided for me. You are the Lord, my provider, and I trust you with my whole heart!

Just Advance the Kingdom!

As I recently strolled through one of our local malls, I walked by a jewelry store with some of the most beautiful diamond earrings I had ever seen. Oh ... were they lovely! I knew I couldn't buy them, because my husband and I had determined that we would focus on investing in the Kingdom of God and blessing others. Our determined purpose was to allow God to add to our lives. Anything that is given will not come by the sweat of our brow, but as a result of God's goodness. It sounds spiritual now, but in agony I turned my back on that lovely array of diamonds. Even though my back was turned, my heart continued to reach, but in compliance I sadly walked away.

With each step away from the store, my mind started to engage. I was mentally struggling with the thought that I have always had to put other things and people before myself. By the time I reached my car, I was fuming. The thought of praying for the earrings had never crossed my mind. I never said a word. I just got into the car and drove off to my "wonderful little always taking care of others life!" Enough said.

God has a way. He has a system by which He wants our lives to operate. Fortunately, His system is vastly different from that of the world. In the world, it's "take all you can get." In the Kingdom of God, it's "give all you can take." They are complete opposites. The world says, "Hate those who hate you." The Kingdom says, "Love those who hate you."

The world seeks after things. It's a lot like the little girl in *Willy Wonka & the Chocolate Factory*. Violet wanted the world. She wanted the whole world, and she wanted it now! As a believer, we can't be like Violet. We are not to seek after the things of this world. The Bible tells us not to love the world or the things in the world. We can have them, but they can't have us. Our love has to be directed toward God, and our seeking is for the advancement of His Kingdom. God promised in Matthew 6:30–33 to add things to our lives if we *first* seek His Kingdom.

If God cares so wonderfully for the wildflowers that are here today and thrown into the fire tomorrow, he will certainly care for you. Why do you have so little faith? So don't worry about these things saying, "What will we eat? What will we drink? What will we wear?" These things dominate the thoughts of the unbelievers, but your Heavenly Father already knows all your needs. Seek the Kingdom of God above all else, and live righteously, and He will give you everything you need. (Matthew 6:30–33 NLT)

This is the verse of scripture that came to me that day when I was having a meltdown as I drove away from the mall. A lot of times we know the Word, but our problem is not in *knowing* the Word, it's in *doing* the Word. We have to do what God says in order to reap the benefits of Matthew 6:33. If "everything you need" has not been given, then check out your seek.

What are you reaching for? Where have you placed your affections? Wherever your affections go, there also goes your heart. Are the majority of your efforts spent on obtaining things? Are you content with what you have until God adds more to your life? Are your efforts on advancing God's Kingdom? When you give your time, resources, and attention to promoting God's agenda, God will just "add" things to your life, and you will find you rarely have to pray about "things" because they just come to you. And they do so in the most amazing ways.

I was recently traveling to a ministry engagement, and as I walked to my gate at the airport, I ran into some long-time friends. We embraced and they said, "Melva, we have been thinking about you for some time now and were hoping that we would see you soon. We have something that we believe God wants you to have." Guess what they gave me? A beautiful pair of *diamond earrings!* God did exactly what He said He would do. He *gave* me the desire of my heart (Psalms 37:4).

Let your advancement of the Kingdom increase and bless you today. God can do it in places and ways you can't even imagine! Including the airport! My goodness! Who carries diamond earrings around hoping to see someone? Only those whom God has chosen to carry blessings for your life. He'll do it for you, too! Have a great day!

Today's Scriptures: Matthew 6:30–33; Psalms 37:4.

Today's Prayer/Confession: Today I will seek first the Kingdom of God, living righteously, and He will give me everything that I need. I commit my time, resources, and attention to advancing His Kingdom.

Change Begins with Me!

This morning I woke up thinking about the areas of my life that need to change. These areas are within my heart as well as in my natural day-to-day life. There are attitudes, mindsets, and situations that have the potential to negatively impact who I am and where I desire to go in life. Sometimes I get frustrated with myself because I know that there is a way for me to achieve all that I desire, but because of a lack of discipline, courage, or knowledge, I allow myself to be held back. I think I speak for many. Recently I found myself saying, "Lord, I want to change." But where does change begin?

When it comes to change, whether it's changing your eating habits, your financial situation, your spiritual condition, your educational level, or your life as a whole, it will not happen until you make it happen. I spent many, many years looking up in the sky wondering when God was going to make His move on me. It was almost like I was looking for Him to be my fairy godmother, who would one day come and transform me into a beautiful, spiritual princess.

I eventually began to realize that God had already made His move when He redeemed me through the blood of Christ. So He was waiting on me. I was looking at Him, and He was looking at me. Consequently, I didn't change. One day I was reading the book of Ephesians and read all the way through to Colossians. And I saw it just as clear as day! In those passages, Paul kept using words like *let, don't, do,* and *you.* These words indicated that I was the responsible party. I had to do something if I wanted my life to change. Here I had waited for years for God to change me and my life situation. But reading through this passage, I saw that neither I nor my situation would change until *I* did something. Yes, it is God's power that ultimately makes the change, but I am the initiator of the change. I had to do something first.

Armed and ready for battle, I went "cold turkey" in a lot of areas and quickly became frustrated because I only changed for a period of time. Before long, I was right back doing or acting like I said I wouldn't. Why? I was trying to change my actions without changing my way of thinking, and this is impossible. You will never change your life if you don't change the way you think. The Bible puts it this way: *"Don't copy the behavior and customs of this world,* **but let God transform you into a new person by changing the way you think.** *Then you will know what God wants you to do, and you will know how good and pleasing and perfect his will really is"* (Romans 12:2 NLT—emphasis mine).

In order for your life to blossom, you will have to take on the challenge of changing your thought processes. There are so many people who would be a success in life if they didn't think the way they did. If your thoughts are bad or negative, your actions will be bad or negative. You can only produce outwardly what you are inwardly. And even if you don't completely act out your thoughts, they will still impact your life.

God wants us to use His Word to transform our thinking. The word *transform* is the same word as *metamorphose*; it means to change you in a way that turns you into another being, like a caterpillar into a butterfly. If you really want your life to change, you are going to have to take the necessary time to feed on the Word of God and then act on what you receive. Feeding will give you knowledge, but acting after you have fed brings transformation. Start today, and as you do, you will be changed into the person that you've always wanted to be.

God bless you and have a wonderful day!

Today's Scripture: Romans 12:2.

Today's Prayer/Confession: Today I will allow the Word of God to transform me into the person that God has ordained me to be. Change begins with me!

Forgive Yourself

Every one of us has a past, and every one of us has something that God has delivered us from. As a pastor and biblical counselor, I've witnessed firsthand the challenge many of us have letting go of our past mistakes. Though they accept Jesus as Lord of their lives, they struggle to accept His love and forgiving power. The Word of God clearly tells us that we have been forgiven. Colossians 1:14 states: *"In whom we have redemption through his blood, even the forgiveness of sins."* The word *redemption* in this passage means we have been released and the ransom has been paid.

Jesus paid the penalty for every wrong act and sin you and I will ever commit, and He did it with His own blood. God forgives us because of the blood of Jesus, and it doesn't matter what we have done. If we walk in the light of the Word of God, the power in His blood will cleanse us and give us a fresh, new life.

But if we walk in the light, as he is in the light, we have fellowship one with another, and the blood of Jesus Christ his Son cleanseth us from all sin (1 John 1:7). God has forgiven you! He is not mad at you or holding a grudge against you. He loves you and wants you to receive all He has provided through the blood of Jesus. This is what the plan of redemption is all about. It provided the way to walk free of your sin and past mistakes and become a new person.

If any man be in Christ he is a new species of being, (one that never existed before), look, old things have passed away and everything has become new (2 Corinthians 5:17 Amplified).

You are a new creation right now! God has forgiven you! Forgive yourself and don't be your own worst enemy. You have enough against you—negative people as well as Satan, who is the accuser of the brethren. He's the one who stands before God constantly throwing up your mistakes. But Jesus stands as your intercessor (Hebrews 7:25) or your "lawyer." He tells the Father on every occasion, "Father, I died for that. They are redeemed and forgiven because of the price I paid. My blood was shed for them. They are not guilty."

Use the power in the blood of Jesus and recognize what God has done for you. When thoughts of the past try to weigh you down, say, "I'm forgiven! Jesus died for that, and I am a new creature in Christ." Don't dishonor what He has done for you by holding on to the mistakes of your past. Let go of the past and unleash the potential to be the person God has created you to be. He loves you, and *you are forgiven*!

Today's Scriptures: Colossians 1:14; 1 John 1:7; 2 Corinthians 5:17; Hebrews 7:25.

Today's Prayer/Confession: I will not allow my past to hold me back. God has forgiven me so I can forgive myself. I am free from the mistakes of the past and I'm not looking back. I'm moving forward, in Jesus's name!

Raise the Roof on Your Thinking!

I once heard a story about a man sent as a representative to another country. When he arrived, he did business with an extremely wealthy man. When the time came for the representative to leave, the wealthy man's servant said, "In our country it is customary to give a gift to show our appreciation. What can I give you?" The representative told the wealthy man that giving him a gift wouldn't be necessary, but the man insisted. After going back and forth, the representative finally gave in and said, "Well all right, give me ah ... a golf club."

The wealthy man said, "A golf club?"

The representative replied, "Yes, a golf club."

"Okay," the wealthy man said.

The representative boarded a plane and went back to his country. Several weeks later there was a knock at his door. When the representative opened the door, the servant of the wealthy man was standing before him saying, "I've come to take you to your golf club." To the representative's amazement, the wealthy man had purchased a multimillion dollar golf resort for him. Although both had heard "golf club," what was in the mind of one was totally different from what was in the mind of the other. One man thought on a small scale. The image in his mind was an apparatus used to hit golf balls on the green. The other man thought on an entirely different level. The image in his mind was a full-fledged golf club resort, with lakes and plenty of land—same words, different perceptions.

Your perception determines how far you will advance in life. In Isaiah 55:8–9, God made this statement: *"My thoughts are higher than your thoughts, and my ways are higher than your ways."* Yes, it's true that God's thoughts are higher than ours, but He gave us the mind of Christ and His Word so we have access to His thoughts. God's thoughts are higher than ours, but not inaccessible.

How do you perceive the will of God for your life? Do you believe God will bless you beyond measure so you can advance His kingdom and bless others? Or do you just want to get your bills paid? In the days we are living in, we have to "raise the roof" on our thinking. You serve a big God who wants to do big things in a big way, and He wants to do them through you. This is foreign to many Christians, but it's the truth. There is untapped potential in every one of us, and we can't be afraid to step out beyond our level of comfort.

In Genesis 15, all Abraham wanted was a son, but God wanted to give him nations. So God had to raise his level of thinking. He told Abraham to come out of his tent and look up, look out, and look beyond. In other words, God was telling Abraham, "What I have for you is *too big* to be contained in this little tent." A tent is a place of confinement. It has limitations. God wanted Abraham to take the limits off so that he could see beyond his current circumstances.

The Word of the Lord to you today is this: **Don't limit God, and don't limit yourself by small thinking.**

If you think small, you will accomplish small things because it is impossible to live beyond your own mental capacity. Proverbs 23:7 (NKJV) says: *"For as he thinks in his heart, so is he."* If you think small, you will be small. Think big! There are too many Christians afraid to take godly risks. They don't like to rock any boats and end up taking the God-sized vision within them and condensing it into something practical or comfortable. God's vision is too big to stay in a tent! If what you are endeavoring to accomplish in life is something easily attainable, it's not God. All that God wants you to do in life, every task and endeavor, is bigger than you are. All He is looking for is someone who will dare to live by faith and trust Him to bring it to pass. Are you that one?

When you raise your level of thinking by constantly meditating and speaking the Word of God, then, and only then, will you begin to see the plan of God unfold in a big way in your life.

God bless you today!

Today's Scriptures: Isaiah 55:8–9; Genesis 15; Proverbs 23:7.

Today's Prayer/Confession: God, you are in me doing big things in a big way. Today I align my thoughts with yours, and I will rise to your level of thinking according to the Word of God!

Don't Be Cold and Unresponsive

Many years ago I met a man at a convention who seemed "over the top" in my opinion. Every time we encountered him, he was full of what appeared to be joy. He would say in the most annoying way, "Amen, Brother, Amen, Sister. Glory to God!" We would have to stand and listen to him go on and on about all the things he possessed and his latest conversations with God. It happened so often that I would beg my husband to turn and go in another direction if we saw him coming. If I couldn't get away, I would stand there, cold and unresponsive, as my husband and the man conversed.

One day, as I was in prayer about a particular situation, I heard these words in my heart, "You are jealous of his accomplishments and his level of spiritual maturity. Repent and embrace him." Although I was praying about something else, I knew exactly what that meant. I repented right there on the spot and did what God instructed. Now he is a ministry friend.

Too often we judge people because they may not act or respond like we do. I've noticed that carnal Christians get easily envious of spiritual Christians, and spiritual Christians get irritated and pull away from carnal Christians. Both end up acting as I did—cold and unresponsive.

The Body of Christ is a body. God designed it to function in harmony. When we allow division and separation among us, it stops the flow of the power of God in our lives. Satan wants nothing more than to pull us apart, judging one another instead of loving and embracing each other. I've met scores of men and women who have siblings and don't get along with them for one reason or another. They go years without conversing or interacting and the family is devastated. The same thing is happening in the Body of Christ, and God wants this to end.

In Proverbs 6:16–19, there is a list of six things God hates, but there is a seventh thing that is called an abomination, "*he that soweth discord among brethren.*" The word *abomination* comes from a Greek word that means "a disgusting thing," so when we allow ourselves to divide and separate, it is disgusting to God. We are His children. He loves us and He wants us to love each other. There are so many who won't interact with others because of how they were made to feel. Let's turn this around and determine to do our best to love people, no matter what they may have done. It's not easy, but God has given us the ability to do it, so we can.

Today you may have someone in your life that you have become cold and unresponsive to. I want to encourage you to pray for that individual and do your absolute best to embrace and open your heart to him or her. When you embrace that person, the love of God will begin to flow through you and eventually shatter what stands between you. Do all you can to follow peace with *all* men, and as a result, you will be able to see the Lord in operation in your life (Hebrews 12:14).

Have a wonderful day!

Today's Scriptures: Proverbs 6:16–19; Hebrews 12:14.

Today's Prayer/Confession: Father, help me to embrace those who may not be as I am and to love as you love. If there is any cold and unresponsive behavior in me, I repent and ask you to forgive me. Thank you for helping me and/or forgiving me, in Jesus's name, Amen.

Recognize Your Enemy

When people look at your life from the outside, they can't see that there have been great battles fought and forces overcome. In everyone's life, there will be strategic conflicts and situations designed by the enemy to "take you out." The attempt to take us out may be experienced at a physical, mental, or spiritual level. It is determined by the part of you that the adversary gains access to. I'm not glorifying him, but Satan is shrewd. He will set up an entire sitcom with many episodes and you playing the starring role in order to watch you fall.

This is why Jesus told us in Matthew 10:16 to be *"wise as serpents and harmless as doves."* If they don't operate in godly wisdom, even the most spiritual individuals among us can be duped and find themselves on the ground looking up. Satan is a real enemy, and he is on a real mission to bring destruction to your very real life. Thank God 2 Corinthians 2:14 states that God always causes us to triumph through our Lord Jesus Christ! So we should not fear Satan.

One of the greatest weapons in the enemy's arsenal is the atomic bomb called "My fight is with Flesh and Blood." Unfortunately, this weapon is used every single day, and the world is full of casualties from this single weapon. Some are in critical care, some are badly wounded, and some have lost their lives. The impact of this weapon is so severe that it has destroyed entire churches, ruined relationships, and devastated many families. It is detonated when Satan is able to deceive us into thinking that our fight is against one another instead of against him. This is why we have to stay on our knees and in the Word of God so we can clearly see who our enemy really is.

When my oldest son, Quenton, was seventeen, we got into a very heated debate. I was on my way to the place of full detonation when suddenly the Word of the Lord came floating up in my heart saying, "He's not the enemy, and your fight is not with Quenton. Your fight is with the enemy that is influencing him. Now take authority over this situation and speak to the enemy behind him and this will change." Now, I'm sure Quenton thought I had lost my mind, because my facial expression and the direction of my words instantly changed. I began to command the enemy to take his hands off my son and leave my home. Within minutes,

Quenton was in tears, asking me to forgive him. We hugged and I brushed my hair back down and went back to washing the dishes.

I, like many of you, thought my issue was a person, when in actuality it was the enemy influencing him. He wasn't "possessed" by the devil, but he was influenced by him. The enemy brings thoughts, ideas, and suggestions to people, and if they are not spirit-filled or spirit-led, they will yield to his voice. Before you know it, you'll be in an all-out war with them instead of with your real enemy. Ephesians 6:12 says this: *"For we wrestle not against flesh and blood, but against principalities, against powers, against the rulers of the darkness of this world, against spiritual wickedness in high places."*

I'm not implying that every negative encounter you have will be inspired by the devil. Some are just personality conflicts, so please don't think there is a devil in every person you have a challenge with. But one of the greatest gifts you can give yourself is recognizing who your real adversary is. It is not your wife, husband, children, boss, or pastor. It is spiritual forces designed to "take you out," and they will do so by any means necessary if you fail to walk in your God-given authority. They will use anyone in your sphere of influence who will listen to them, and they are no respecters of persons.

This is why we have to be quick to forgive and slow to respond when people mistreat us. When we react in our flesh instead of responding out of love, it clouds our ability to see who we are fighting, and Satan can get an advantage over us. *"To whom ye forgive anything, I forgive also: for if I forgave anything, to whom I forgave it, for your sakes forgave I it in the person of Christ; Lest Satan should get an advantage of us: for we are not ignorant of his devices"* (2 Corinthians 2:10–11). Verse 11 in the NIRV reads like this: *"We don't want Satan to outsmart us. We know how he does his evil work."*

You have victory over every situation that you may face, but victory has conditions. Jesus said in Luke 6 that you must love those who hate you, pray for those who hurt you, and do good to those who mistreat you. When you do these things, you give God something to work with and position yourself to stand in a place of victory. Let's not fight each other.

God bless you. Have a wonderful day!

Today's Scriptures: Matthew 10:16; 2 Corinthians 2:14; Ephesians 6:12; 2 Corinthians 2:10–11; Luke 6.

Today's Prayer/Confession: I am not ignorant of the wicked schemes and strategies of the devil. I'm wise as a serpent and harmless as a dove. I have the power of Christ dwelling in me, and I walk in the Love of God and reign in victory through my Lord and Savior Jesus Christ!

The Life You Live

The Word of the Lord for today is this: "The life you live before your children will be the life lived through your children."

"Ye are our epistle written in our hearts, known and read of all men" (2 Corinthians 3:2). A lot of times we think 2 Corinthians 3:2 applies only to those of us on our jobs, at church, or at places where we encounter adults, but the scripture says "all men," which includes our children. Whether we like it or not, what we do or don't do before our children is going to be repeated before others. In the Old Testament, God repeatedly made reference to the children of the Israelites. He gave specific instructions on how the children were to be taught. The directives given were to be handed down from generation to generation because God wanted an entire lineage of people who would walk with Him, not just a single generation. The instructions were to be lived out in front of the children.

What you find in Christendom is adult believers who separate their walk with God from their walk with their children, but our children are to be an intricate part of our lives with God. Your daily walk with Christ should translate into something that your children can see and experience. I was studying the life of Abram (Abraham) and found something interesting from the Hebrew writings. Abram's father was an idol worshipper; no doubt, as a child, Abram was, too.

But something happened to Abram when he was very young. It is said that at the age of ten, Abram went to live with Noah, who was 892 years old when Abram was born. It was during this time that Abram began to hunger for God instead of the ways of his father. What happened? Abram spent many years under the tutelage of Noah. Genesis 6:9 says that Noah was a just and perfect man, and he walked with God all his generations. Abram walked with Noah, Noah walked with God, and therefore Abram walked with God. Noah's life lived out before Abram created within him a hunger for God. What kind of hunger is your lifestyle creating within your children?

Just like the Israelites, God wants our children to know Him and to walk with Him. So we have to make sure that our lives are living examples of Christ. You should want your children to love your God more than you love Him, and that will happen when they can see God in operation and in manifestation in your own life.

I was raised by a praying, Bible-reading grandmother. She loved the Word of God and would have books and Bibles all over her bed every night. When our youngest daughter Kayla was five or six years old, I began to notice all the Bibles and journals around her bed each morning. I didn't think much about it and just moved them out of the way. One day as I was making my bed, I found myself moving my own books, Bibles, and journals. Then it dawned on me—Kayla watched me, I watched my grandmother—the cycle was continuing.

If you have lived a life that you don't want repeated through your children, it's not too late to change. Don't trouble yourself with your past, but endeavor to be the example that you have been called to be today. God loves you. He has made a way for you to change the course of your life and the lives of your children.

Therefore shall ye lay up these my words in your heart and in your soul, and bind them for a sign upon your hand, that they may be as frontlets between your eyes. And ye shall teach them your children, speaking of them when thou sittest in thine house, and when thou walkest by the way, when thou liest down, and when thou risest up. And thou shalt write them upon the door posts of thine house, and upon thy gates: That your days may be multiplied, and the days of your children, in the land which the LORD sware unto your fathers to give them, as the days of heaven upon the earth. (Deuteronomy 11:18–21)

Today's Scriptures: 2 Corinthians 3:2; Genesis 6:9; Deuteronomy 11:18–21.

Today's Prayer/Confession: Father, today I commit to living a life that will draw my children closer to you. Help me to remember that I am a living example of your grace and power on the earth. May my life be pleasing to you, and may my children love you all the days of their lives, in Jesus's name, Amen.

Open Your Mouth and Ask

Deep in the crevices of my heart, I have a place filled with situations, people, places, and things that need to be prayed about or prayed out. They are just sitting in what I liken to a waiting room, waiting for the opportunity to come forward. They are not like those situations that I simply throw up toward heaven while I'm doing laundry or taking the kids to school. These only seem to come from the waiting room when I've quieted myself in times of prayer and/or fasting. They won't move until I open my mouth and call their name.

Jesus said this in John 15:7: "*If ye abide in me, and my words abide in you, ye shall* **ask** *what ye will, and it shall be done unto you.*" The word *ask* in this context is used over fifty times in the gospels. This is important because a lot of people leave this vital ingredient out of their times of prayer. They won't open their mouths and ask God to move in a particular situation. They reason that He already knows, so it's not necessary to ask, but what they fail to realize is although God knows about it, He won't move solely on the knowledge of it. He has designed the Kingdom in such a way that you must ask. Unfortunately, when you fail to ask, the waiting room of your heart stays full.

A lot of people think they have prayed about a situation because they went to God and vented or cried. Although somewhat relieved, their hearts remain heavy and prayers remain unanswered. This is because they haven't really asked for anything. They just complained or had an emotional release, and neither will bring results.

Ask in the Greek means "to call for." It gives the implication that whatever is desired must be called for or called out of the invisible realm into the visible. When I need my children for a particular reason, I call for them to come to where I am. If they hear me, they know they are to respond at the first call. This is exactly the way it is with our times of asking.

God has given us authority on the earth, and He expects us to "call for" the things and situations we desire on the earth. Our focus must be on calling, not complaining or venting. When we ask in line with the Word of God, we operate on the earth as God does. Romans 4:17 says, "*God* **calleth** *those things that be not as though they were.*" Act as God does.

You were created in His image and likeness, so instead of saying what you see, call for what you want to see. In the place of lack, call for abundance. In the place of sickness, call for divine health and healing. In the place of trouble, call for peace.

In closing, James 4:2–3 says: "*Ye have not, because ye ask not. Ye ask, and receive not, because ye ask amiss, that ye may consume it upon your lusts.*" If we use our definition for *ask,* it would sound like this, "You have not because you "call for" not. You "call for" and receive not because you "call for" amiss, that you may consume it upon your lust." The word *amiss* means "to speak ill of." In other words, you don't receive when you "call for" because you are speaking ill of a person or a situation in order to benefit yourself. And with God this won't do. Motive is everything. Use your time wisely. God already knows how bad it is, but He doesn't want the bad glorified. Don't use your time or tongue to speak ill. Keep your heart right, and never underestimate the power of asking.

God bless you! Have a powerful day!

Today's Scriptures: John 15:7; Romans 4:17; James 4:2–3.

Today's Prayer/Confession: Today I will use the power of asking to bring forth those things that I desire on the earth. I will not use my time of asking wastefully, but I will pull out of the unseen realm these things that will glorify the Father, In Jesus's name, Amen!

Checks and Balances

Why do we do what we do? Behind every action there is a motive, a drive, or an objective, and it's our duty to ensure our motives are always pure. If we find ourselves making decisions out of selfishness, pride, or fear, the root is usually a wrong motive. We all need a way to measure why we do what we do, and this measurement helps keep balance in our lives. It can be dangerous when one part of who we are is granted too much leeway or power. There has to be an internal system of accountability that sets off an alarm when we are making or moving on decisions for the wrong reason. Sometimes we may feel justified in our actions—we may feel we have the right to think, feel, or even act a particular way. But if our actions are not rooted in the love of God, they can become detrimental to our lives.

Proverbs 16:2 says that we can be pure in our own eyes, but God examines our motives. God's eye is always on our heart, watching not just what we do, but why we do what we do. His Spirit and His Word are the check and balance of life.

There is a system in our country known as "checks and balances." The three branches of our government all have certain powers. However, checks and balances ensure that one branch does not exercise too much of that power. Are wrong motives exercising too much power in your life? We all need checks and balances. No matter what may be going on in life, it's our responsibility to make sure everything is done from a place of love. It doesn't matter what it may be. Love has to be the foundation for it all, and when it is, our decision making will always flow from a pure place.

In the early days of our marriage my husband was managing a business that paid him very well. During that time, we shared a joint checking account. Each pay period, I rode his back about excessive spending and the fact that God wanted him to be a good steward. It was so intense at times it brought great tension into our home. In my mind it was justifiable. I thought I was doing right. But one day in prayer, I was talking to the Lord about something unrelated and had a flashback to my going in and out of women's clothing stores spending his money. Suddenly into my heart came these words: "Your motive is wrong. You're putting pressure on him so you can have exclusive access to his money. As long as you operate here, I cannot bless you. Now repent and go to him and apologize." Oh, I can't tell you how hard it was for me. If I confessed, I would lose it all, and the idea that I couldn't buy what I wanted when I wanted tore me up inside. Believe it or not, how I felt about losing access to the money—not the Lord's exposing me—was the proof I needed to reveal my wrong motives.

I apologized, and for a period of time, I gave him a monthly stipend out of my own money just to conquer that spirit of selfishness in my life. In Psalms 26:2 (NLT), David prayed this: *"Put me on trial, Lord, and cross-examine me. Test my motives and my heart."* As believers, we have the responsibility to keep our motives before the Lord. This is why the Word of God is essential. Hebrews 4:12 calls it the discerner between the thoughts and intents of the heart. In other words, the Word of God will reveal to us where our motives lie, and if you discover yours to be impure or selfishly driven, repent and make things right. God loves you.

Today as you feed on God's Word, allow the Word to show you your heart. God bless you!

Today's Scriptures: Proverbs 16:2; Psalms 26:2; Hebrews 4:12.

Today's Prayer/Confession: Father, today I will allow you to search and examine my heart and test my motives. Show me any hidden thing that is not of you. I will bring it into a place of subjection and uprightness. In Jesus's name, Amen!

Don't Let the Dream in You Die

When I started writing this morning, before one word hit the page, the sheet of paper in front of me was white, clean, and clear. The white paper is like a canvas waiting for the painter to create something wonderful that he and others can enjoy. The paper represents opportunity.

When you accepted Jesus as your Lord and Savior, your life was like that white sheet of paper, clean and clear. The most powerful thing is the fact that you get the opportunity to be the painter of your own life. I know that ultimately God is the Divine Painter, the Master Craftsman, but He gives us opportunities, gifts, and talents, and we can use them to open great doors of blessing for our lives.

Every good gift and every perfect gift is from above, and cometh down from the Father of lights, with whom is no variableness, neither shadow of turning (James 1:17).

At birth, you came into the world with gifts, and these gifts were given by God. What you do with your gift is entirely up to you. The late Kenneth E. Hagin made this statement: "Many people live and die and never enter into the first phase of the ministry that God has for them." I believe this holds true for gifts also. Many people live and die, never allowing the gift that is within them the freedom of expression.

Some of you reading this devotional right now are sitting with great potential inside of you, but you are afraid to step out. You are afraid of being rejected, afraid of what others might say, afraid of the unknown, afraid of what it might cost. Instead of pursuing the greatness God has placed within you, you make the choice to sit on the sidelines of life, watching others cruise by fulfilling their life dreams. Don't let the gift lie dormant, and don't allow the dreams or visions God has placed in you die! He put them within you so they could come out of you. What are you doing with what is in you?

Several years ago, I went to Chicago with a friend to celebrate her birthday. We worked for the same company. While standing on Michigan Avenue she said, "Melva, God never intended for you to fulfill another man's vision and let your vision die. What are you doing with all that's in you? Are you going to forget what God has placed within you?" I stood there weeping. To be honest, I hadn't thought about myself. Without realizing it, I had spent much of my adult life serving someone else's vision and never even thought about fulfilling my own. I was content where I was. It was comfortable, but it wasn't all God had for me.

It is said that every person will have one opportunity in life to become independently wealthy. I don't know if that's true or not, but what if it is? Did you pass yours up? If I don't know anything else, I know our place of wealth is connected to the gift deep within us, and when we can connect our God-given passions with our God-given gifts, it's over! The flood gates are going to open for us, and the provision of God will be ours for the taking. Don't let the dream in you die. Pray and ask the Lord to show you creative ways to get the gift inside of you out for others to enjoy!

God bless you and have a powerful day!

Today's Scriptures: James 1:17; Proverbs 13:12.

Today's Prayer/Confession: I acknowledge the gift of God within me. I won't allow my dreams and passions to die while I advance someone else's vision. God's vision in and for me is great, and it will come to pass in my lifetime!

Spiritual Bumpers

I once had a daydream that impacted my life and ministered truth to my spirit. I was walking down a sidewalk and started to veer off to the left, getting close to the edge of the street, when the Spirit of God surrounded me and gently led me back to the middle of the sidewalk. As I continued walking, the same thing happened on the right side of the road. But each time I veered off, the Spirit of God led me back to where I needed to be.

If we are not watchful, we can sometimes find ourselves veering off in life. One of the many jobs of the Holy Spirit is to help keep our lives in line with the will of God. I can't begin to tell you how many times I've had to be led, directed, or even pushed back to the middle of the road. The middle of the road represents the will of God for our lives. It's what the Clark Sisters in the seventies called "the safest place in the whole wide world."

There are many believers who are in a constant tizzy worrying about the will of God for their lives. They place great stress on themselves because they are afraid they have missed, or might miss, His will. However, God knows how to get you down the path He has designed for your life. He knows how to direct you so that you live smack-dab in the middle of His will, His plan, and His purpose. It is similar to go-carting. When you're driving your go-cart, it is completely padded, and when the car hits a wall, it goes back toward the center of the track. You have spiritual bumpers, and God, as the Holy Spirit, uses those bumpers to keep you where you need to be.

Over twenty years ago, I sensed I was to attend Bible School, but I didn't know what to do. I was a single mom with twins, and life was comfortable for me. I had a very good job, a nice home, and the support of family and friends. Leaving was a major decision, because I would uproot my children and move to a city with no home, no job, and no family or friends. I needed God to show me what to do. I read Psalms 119:105, but I didn't get it. My mind could not wrap around the idea of the Bible telling me what to do, but in childlike faith I told God, "I don't know how this works, but I trust you. So I'm going to look at this verse until I know what to do."

For weeks, I spoke the scripture out loud and silently. I looked at the scripture every chance I had. Then one day, the knowledge of God came and His plan was laid out before me. In my heart I knew exactly what to do, timeframe and all. With that knowing came an enormous amount of peace, so I acted on it. Within six months, I was in Bible School, with my kids in school, and on my way to being trained for the ministry. That was over twenty years ago, but it is how I still operate in life today. If it worked for me, it will work for you.

"For as many as are led by the Spirit of God, they are the sons of God" (Romans 8:14).

If you have a decision to make, don't move quickly. Sometimes the leading of the Spirit is very subtle. It is just an inward knowing that "this is where I should be" or "this is where I should go." Pull away and meditate on the Word of God, allowing His spiritual bumpers to lead you in life.

God bless you today!

Today's Scriptures: Psalms 119:105; Romans 8:14.

Today's Prayer/Confession: Today I will meditate on God's Word. I will acknowledge Him in ALL of my ways, and He will make straight and plain my path. I know what to do because the Holy Spirit of God reveals God's will for me.

Keep Your Heart Right

Keeping your heart in the right place will be one of the many tasks you will find yourself engaging in every day. As a believer, if your heart gets out of whack, your actions will eventually follow. Proverbs 4:23 tells us: *"Keep thy heart with all diligence; for out of it are the issues of life."* The Message says: *"Keep vigilant watch over your heart, that's where life starts."* Good life or bad life, it all begins with the heart.

We each have the responsibility of developing and protecting our own heart. Much like the brain is to the human body, the heart is a control center for your life. If unprotected it becomes the gateway to contamination. And a contaminated heart will negatively impact your life. Matthew 15:18–19 (The Message) says: *"But what comes out of the mouth gets its start in the heart. It's from the heart that we vomit up evil arguments, murders, adulteries, fornications, thefts, lies, and cussing. That's what pollutes."*

Jesus said it is what comes out of the heart that makes one unclean. Everything begins in the heart long before it ever manifests anywhere else. If the heart is not constantly being checked by the Word of God, it has the potential to become what the Bible calls *defiled*, which means "unclean and impure." Protecting the heart is the process of keeping guard over what goes into it through the ear gate, eye gate, or mental gate.

The biggest point of entry is through the mental gate, because Satan has access to the mental realm. He can bring thoughts to our minds, and if we meditate on them long enough, they will eventually work their way into our hearts and affect our lives. The ear and eye gate work with the mental gate. They transmit images and information to the mind. From there the information filters its way into the heart. So your heart must be protected at all times.

As you go throughout your day, keep vigilant watch over what you see, hear, and think!

God bless you!

Today's Scriptures: Proverbs 4:23; Matthew 15:18–19.

Today's Prayer/Confession: I will keep a vigilant watch over my heart to make sure all that I do brings glory to God.

The Abiding Word

Prior to the birth of my last two children, I would spend hours reading the Word of God to them. When they were born, I placed CD players in their room and played healing scriptures throughout the night in order to keep the Word in their atmosphere. My son, Kyle, is so accustomed to having the scriptures played that when he attends a sleepover, he packs a CD with his healing scriptures. To this day, it is rare he is ever found asleep without them.

My daughter, Kayla, started out with the scriptures exactly as her brother did, but when she got old enough to voice her opinion, she would yell throughout the house, "The Word of God is too loud!" I didn't want to disturb her sleep, so I found myself reducing the volume in her room until eventually the day came when I noticed she wasn't listening to the scriptures at all. The Holy Spirit brought to my attention that from the time Kayla stopped listening to her healing scriptures, she had been hospitalized several times and had missed a significant number of days from school because of frequent illnesses. Kyle, on the other hand, has rarely had so much as a common cold.

What has made the difference? The difference is abiding in the Word of God. John 1:1–4 says: *"In the beginning was the Word, and the Word was with God, and the Word was God. The same was in the beginning with God. All things were made by him; and without him was not anything made that was made. In him was life; and the life was the light of men."* By careful study of this passage, it is safe to conclude that the Word is referring to Jesus! Jesus and the Word are synonymous.

In John 15:4, Jesus made this statement: *"Abide in me, and I in you. As the branch cannot bear fruit of itself, except it abide in the vine; no more can ye, except ye abide in me."* We could read the passage like this: "Abide in the Word and the Word will abide in you. As a branch cannot bear fruit by itself, except it abide in the Word; no more can you, except you abide in the Word." This is a very powerful statement! It reveals why many fail to bear fruit in so many areas of their lives.

Even though the times Kayla listened to the healing scriptures weren't the only times she received the Word of God, it was the time she received concentrated doses, and as a result she bore healing fruit. Proverbs 4:20–22 reveals that the Word of God is health to all our flesh. *"My son, attend to my words; incline thine ear unto my sayings. Let them not depart from thine eyes; keep them in the midst of thine heart. For they are life unto those that find them, and health to all their flesh."* In other translations the word *health* is replaced with the word *medicine.* God's word is medicine to our flesh.

Healing, along with all the other promises of God, belongs to us. It is our covenant right given by God through the cross of Christ. But in order to receive them, we have to abide in the Word and allow the Word to abide in us. The abiding Word produces results. It reveals the promises of God and releases the power of faith so we can receive.

When we spend time feeding on the Word, absorbing and taking it in, it strengthens our faith grip and builds a platform for us to stand on to ask God for whatever we desire. The abiding Word of God becomes our stability, and when we petition God, we know that the ground we stand on is firm because it's His own Word.

If you abide in Me, and My words abide in you, you will ask what you desire, and it SHALL be done for you. (John 15:7 NKJV)

Let today be a day of abiding in the Word. God has promised to do whatever you ask if you abide. He knows that if you abide in His Word, you will only ask for those things that bring glory to Him. So abide in His Word and allow the Word to heal your body and transform your life. God bless you today!

Today's Scriptures: John 1:1–4; John 15:4, 7; Proverbs 4:20–22.

Today's Prayer/Confession: I abide in the Word of God and the Word of God dwells richly in me. As a result, there is a supernatural flow from God to me, and I receive everything that the abiding Word has for me.

Talk to God about It

One morning the Lord said this to me: "Stop going to other people when you have a problem. Bring your problems to me." Instantly I began to think, "If I needed food, I would go to the grocery store. If I needed a haircut, I would go to a beautician. These individuals are skilled in handling the needs that are presented to them, so why would I take problems away from the problem solver?"

One of my greatest struggles as a young Christian was in believing God cared enough about me to be interested in dealing with or hearing my problems. I mean, He's God. He has billions yelling at Him for help, and I just didn't want to be a bother. So I would find someone else to talk to. Eventually I learned that God was interested in the minuet details of my life, but I had trained myself to talk to other people. So when challenges or problems came, I continued to talk to others instead of talking to God.

As therapeutic as we may believe it is talking to others, they are not the solution to our problems. It may take some of the pressure off of our mind, but it will never resolve the issue deep within the heart. That's reserved solely for God. People can cry with us and lend an ear, some can offer great wisdom, but in the end God is the one who can change our circumstance, and He wants us to come to Him. When we go to others, we make them our confidants and take the risk not only of not having our problem resolved, but also of having our business in the hands of someone who may not respect confidentiality. God, on the other hand, can be trusted. He is without question *The Great Confidant*.

I grew up in the church thinking that I was supposed to call for the elders of the church when I was having troubles in my life. But James 5:13–15 says this: *"Is any among you afflicted? Let him pray. Is any merry? Let him sing psalms. Is any sick among you? Let him call for the elders of the church; and let them pray over him, anointing him with oil in the name of the Lord: And the prayer of faith shall save the sick."*

Notice the only time we are instructed to call for the elders of the church is when we are sick, not when we are afflicted. The word *afflicted* in this passage means "suffering hardship or troubles," so during those times we are instructed to pray for ourselves. We have to learn to humble ourselves and trust God to handle the things that trouble us. 1 Peter 5:6–7 says: *"Humble yourselves therefore under the mighty hand of God, that he may exalt you in due time: Casting all your care upon him; for he careth for you."*

The Amplified Bible says it this way: *"Therefore humble yourselves [demote, lower yourselves in your own estimation] under the mighty hand of God, that in due time He may exalt you, Casting the whole of your care [all your anxieties, all your worries, all your concerns, once and for all] on Him, for He cares for you affectionately and cares about you watchfully."* I love this translation because it has a twofold meaning for me. First, I don't have to worry myself with my problems because God will care about them for me. Second, He cares for me personally, and He does so affectionately and watchfully so I can't lose. We have to realize that we are not turning our troubles over to someone who can only listen and do nothing else. Our God listens and then He acts on our behalf. Let Him act for you!

Today's Scriptures: James 5:13-15; 1 Peter 5:6–7.

Today's Prayer/Confession: I will not carry the weight of the world to others. I won't live with anxiety, but I will trust the Lord with all my heart, casting the whole of my cares on Him because He cares for me watchfully and affectionately!

Unforgiveness Is Not a Word

One day I was standing in the kitchen and my eldest daughter walked in saying, "Mom, did you know that "unforgiveness" is not a word?"

I looked at her and said, "Yes, it is."

"No, it isn't," she replied. She then brought a dictionary out to show me that it wasn't there. She also went to dictionary.com and it wasn't there either. I thought, *If it's not in the dictionary, surely it's in the Word of God.* To my amazement, it wasn't there either. The words *forgive, forgiveness,* and *forgiving* are, but there's nothing on unforgiveness.

Unforgiveness is *not* a word. In fact, Microsoft Word has red lines beneath every place I've typed it. All my life, I've heard messages or conversations about unforgiveness, when in actuality, the word doesn't exist. If the Word of God doesn't acknowledge the existence of unforgiveness, why would we choose to live in it?

All of us have been hurt or disappointed by others. Marriages, friendships, and family relationships have become stunted and unable to grow because people struggle to go beyond the memory of someone who hurt them. You may have heard this before, but I'm going to say it again: Failing to forgive others and holding on to the pains of the past doesn't hurt the person you aren't forgiving, it hurts you. Proverbs 17:22 (NKJV) says: *"A broken spirit dries the bones."* That implies an illness.

Many times we don't understand what happens when we don't forgive. I've counseled many who have taken offense with someone (note that offense is *taken*, not given) who hurt them, and when the other person moves on, the one who took offense becomes bitter because the other person's success and/or ability to move forward torments them. It is a terrible place to live. Why would you give someone else that kind of power in your life? "But you don't know what they did to me. You don't understand the depth of my pain." It doesn't matter. If you are born again, you have the power to forgive because God gave it to you when He gave you His Love.

Forgiveness is a spirit that emanates from God. It's an offspring of His love. Romans 5:5 says: *"The love of God is shed abroad in our hearts by the Holy Ghost which is given unto us."* When you choose to forgive, you release the power of God in your life, and that power heals the wounds in your heart.

People have said, "You haven't forgiven if you haven't forgotten." I totally disagree. I have had things happen in my life that I will never forget. I have forgiven the individual or individuals, but I will never forget, because I don't want to position myself to have it happen to me again. When Jesus was dying on the cross, He didn't say, "Father, forgive them and forget this ever happened because they don't know what they are doing." You may never forget what happened to you, but you can certainly live free from the pain of it, and the first step to freedom is choosing to forgive.

When Jesus said in Matthew 6:14, *"If ye forgive men their trespasses, your heavenly Father will also forgive you,"* He was showing us that forgiveness is conditional. Again, forgiveness is an attribute of God and it flows from Him. When we choose not to walk in forgiveness toward others, we are, in essence, rejecting God and closing the door to our own path of forgiveness. Forgiving my neighbor in the eyes of God is the same as God's forgiveness toward me.

To illustrate this, let's picture forgiveness as a bridge that connects us to God and His many blessings for our lives. God has designed it so everyone, including God Himself, has to use this one bridge. If someone offends me, I have to walk the bridge of forgiveness or run the risk of hindering the operation of God's blessing of forgiveness in my own life. If I need God to forgive me, God then uses the bridge of forgiveness based on 1 John 1:9: *"If we confess our sins, he is faithful and just to forgive us our sins, and to cleanse us from all unrighteousness."*

If I reject forgiveness, however, I am rejecting the only path to God's blessing. Nothing can go out and nothing can come in, including God. There is no other way. So in essence, forgiveness cannot flow from me or toward me. This is why Jesus said in Mark 11:26, *"But if ye do not forgive, neither will your Father which is in heaven forgive your trespasses."* God can't get His forgiveness to us because we are choosing not to walk the bridge and embrace forgiveness. It's not that God is sitting in heaven saying, "You won't forgive them so I won't forgive you." He's not like that. God loves you! However, when you reject forgiveness, you reject Him. He wants His blessings to flow in your life, and He knows when you are unwilling to forgive, He cannot walk with you because He is absolute love and forgiveness.

I know firsthand the struggle to release someone of the debt you feel they owe you. When I was a child, I was deeply wounded by a relative, and in anger I asked the Lord not to allow them to leave the earth without first apologizing to me. But as I have grown in my walk with the Father, I've come to realize that it's not as important as I once thought it to be. Today I'm more interested in the individual coming to know Christ so they won't hurt anyone else. Additionally, my success in life is not predicated on an apology from someone who hurt me. God's plan is intact in my life whether I get the apology or not, so I made a choice to let it go and forgive. You can do the same. Don't reject forgiveness. Allow God to make things right for you.

Much love to you and God bless!

Today's Scriptures: Proverbs 17:22; Romans 5:5; Matthew 6:14; 1 John 1:9; Mark 11:26.

Today's Confession/Prayer: Father, Romans 5:5 states that your love has been poured into my heart by the Holy Ghost. Help me to use that love to release forgiveness into the lives of those who have hurt me. I realize you know what they did, and I thank you that you love me enough to take care of those things that concern me. I trust you, Lord, and I choose to do what you have asked of me. As an act of my faith and my will, I forgive those who have hurt me. I pray for them, trusting that you will bring to pass those things necessary to make me the individual you want me to be. In Jesus's name, Amen.

You Are Deeply Loved by God!

I wasn't raised by my mother or my father. Both of my teenage parents left to find themselves when my twin brother and I were newborns, so I was raised by my grandmother. I grew up most of my life feeling like I wasn't worthy of anything, and although I had aunts and uncles who were there for me, not having the love of my own parents left a deep hole in my heart.

One day, I was crying out to God for my natural father when the Lord spoke to my heart saying, "If you will allow your spirit to connect with me, recognizing me as your Spiritual Father, I will show you my love, and you will never long for your natural father again." I can't begin to tell you how those words have changed my life. I immediately began to call God my Father and started acknowledging Him in my day-to-day life. God has done exactly what He said He would do. He has shown me over and over again how much He loves me, and I have never had another day of sadness or loneliness regarding my natural father.

There are so many that have never fully embraced just how much God loves them. Your story may be similar to or worse than mine. You may not have had a grandmother to go to, or you may have been bounced around from foster home to foster home, but no matter what your situation is or may have been, God loves you! Even if you can't see it with your natural eye, it doesn't change the fact that He does. Sometimes it takes someone else unfolding this truth to us for us to come to the realization that we are people who are deeply loved by God. He loves you with all your mistakes. He loves you with all of your inconsistencies. He loves you no matter where you are or what you have done. God loves you! The question is: Do you believe it?

The Word of God says that while you were still a sinner, God sent His Son to die on the cross for you because He loved you so much (Romans 5:8). Ephesians 2:4–5 says that His love was so great for us that even while we were dead in sins, He made us alive so we could come to Him.

This is the answer to those feeling as though they've done so many things wrong that God couldn't love or forgive them. His love was revealed most when we were in sin. There is nothing that you could ever do or say that could stop God from loving and accepting you. God is not like man.

He is consistent. He loved you before you sinned, He loved you while you were sinning, and He loved you after you sinned. However, when you grab hold of the magnitude of His love, you won't want to sin any longer.

If you look back over your life, you will find places where it was nothing but the mercy and love of God that pulled you out or provided for you. Think on these things. You never starved, even if times were lean, because He loved you. If you were homeless, He opened a shelter, just because He loved you. When you should have lost it all, His love kept your family intact. If someone left you, because of His love you were able to start all over again. I could go on and on.

As you go throughout your day, keep the fact that you are loved by God at the forefront of your mind. Say it to yourself over and over again. Whatever you find yourself doing, make yourself think about the fact that God loves you. Think deeply and watch as His love overwhelms your life.

Blessings to you all!

Today's Scriptures: Romans 5:8; Ephesians 2:4–5.

Today's Prayer/Confession: I am loved by God. Because He loves me, I can live my life free of insecurities and feelings of loneliness. Today I acknowledge His love. I will walk in it, talk in it, and live in it!

The Anointing: God's "Yes" within Us

When my husband and I began in ministry, we had no idea we would step into some of the things we have. Everything we have done, when directed by God, was done far beyond our natural ability. It was done through the anointing!

The anointing is an enablement, an empowerment to do what you have been called by God to do. Under the Old Covenant, men were anointed to carry out a specific task. Aaron was anointed to serve as priest in Leviticus 8:12; David was anointed to serve as king in 1 Samuel 16:13; Jesus was anointed to serve as our High Priest based on Hebrews 3:1–2. But did you know that you have also been anointed?

2 Corinthians 1:21 (NIRV) says: *"He makes both us and you stand firm because we belong to Christ. **He anointed us.**"* The Message translation of this scripture calls the anointing "God's 'Yes' within us." I like that. It's God's approval power housed inside of us to do all He has set before us. If you are a business owner, you are anointed to run your business. God's "Yes" is within you. If you are in the ministry, you are anointed to operate with God's "Yes" within you. If you are a stay-at-home parent, you are anointed to train and parent your children because God's "Yes" is within you. There is no task given by God that lacks a distribution of the anointing to carry it out. You have all you need inside of you right now!

My husband and I had the privilege of meeting Chip Brim, a successful former baseball coach who is now a minister. He made us more aware than ever before of the anointing within us. He made a statement that we use to this very day: "I am anointed to preach the gospel on a level that the world and the church are unfamiliar with, all to the glory of God!" My husband and I took that statement and have used it in every arena of our lives. As a result, our marriage, family, business, church, and relationships have not been the same. Something powerful has taken over, and we recognize that "something" to be the anointing.

Just like us, you are anointed! Acknowledge it! Act on it! And you will see the fruit of it in your life. You are anointed to walk out this day on a level that the world is unfamiliar with, all to the glory of God!

Today's Scriptures: Leviticus 8:12; 1 Samuel 16:13; Hebrews 3:1–2; 2 Corinthians 1:21.

Today's Prayer/Confession: I am anointed to _____ on a level that the world and the church are unfamiliar with, all to the Glory of God!

There Remains a Rest for You

I was driving down the street the other day, and as I turned a corner, the Holy Spirit spoke to me and said, "You have to have a Sabbath." As I continued to drive, I started to turn those words over and over in my mind and realized that I had been running every single day for several months. After much thought, I finally came to a place of agreement with the Holy Spirit—I have to have a Sabbath. *Sabbath* in the Hebrew is *"Shabbath,"* and it means "to desist from labors." In simple terms, it means *to rest.*

Genesis is the creation account. It details all God made during a six-day period. Genesis 2:2–3 says this: *"And on the seventh day God ended his work which he had made; and he rested on the seventh day from all his work which he had made. And God blessed the seventh day, and sanctified it: because that in it he had rested from all his work which God created and made."* There is a reason God wanted Moses, the writer of Genesis, to record this information. He wanted us to see that even God himself takes a day off to rest.

Many of us are guilty of going and going, yet never taking the time to stop and rest. There are more than 107 verses of scripture that deal with the Sabbath—the day of rest—and over 70 verses that use the word *rest* in relation to the Sabbath. God is trying to tell us something. Exodus 31:15 says: *"Six days may work be done; but in the seventh is the Sabbath of rest, holy to the LORD: whosoever doeth any work in the Sabbath day, he shall surely be put to death."* God is not a tyrant. He is not saying, "I'll kill you if you don't rest," but He is saying, "If you don't rest, death is inevitable." God made our bodies, so He knows what the body can handle and what it can't. If He says we need to take a day off to rest, we need to take a day off to rest.

In Matthew 11:28, Jesus told us, *"Come unto me all ye that labour and are heavy laden, and I will give you rest."* The word *rest* in this passage means "to permit one to cease from any movement or labor in order to refresh, recover, and collect his strength." This is what God wants for you and me. If we are not watchful, we can fill our days with so much that we lose consciousness of the fact that our bodies must be refreshed and given time to recover from all we are doing. Christians are dying prematurely because they won't take the time to rest. Don't let that be you.

There remaineth therefore a rest to the people of God. For he that is entered into his rest, he also hath ceased from his own works, as God did from his. Let us labour therefore to enter into that rest, lest any man fall after the same example of unbelief (Hebrews 4:9–11).

God has a special place of refreshing just for you. If you are feeling tired, run down, or overworked, take your Sabbath. God made it for you in His original plan at creation. It is your day of rest. The business, family, and ministry will be okay. In fact, they will be better off because you have taken the time to rest your mind and body, quieting yourself so the voice of the Lord becomes clearer and more distinct in your life. Protect yourself. Protect your Sabbath!

God bless you!

Today's Scriptures: Genesis 1; Genesis 2:2–3; Exodus 31:15; Matthew 11:28; Hebrews 4:9–11.

Today's Prayer/Confession: Father, help me to take my day of rest, refreshing my mind and body. Help me to walk in the knowledge you have given me in your Word so that I have the strength to fulfill your plan on the earth. In Jesus's name, Amen!

Speak What You Desire

In Matthew 6:33, Jesus stated that when we seek first the Kingdom of God and His righteousness, food, drink, and clothing will automatically be added unto us. He gave us strict instructions not to worry about "these things" because they will be provided by our Heavenly Father. Does this mean I'm never supposed to ask for anything, but should wait for Him to give me everything? The answer is no.

In Mark 11:22–24, we read:

And Jesus answering saith unto them, Have faith in God. For verily I say unto you, That whosoever shall say unto this mountain, Be thou removed, and be thou cast into the sea; and shall not doubt in his heart, but shall believe that those things which he saith shall come to pass; he shall have whatsoever he saith. Therefore I say unto you, What things soever ye desire, when ye pray, believe that ye receive them, and ye shall have them.

Jesus instructed the disciples to have faith in God. Other translations say, "Have the God kind of faith." What kind of faith does God have? Based on Mark 11, God has mountain-moving faith, and He expects us to have the same.

In my opinion, one of the greatest faith lessons ever taught is found in Genesis chapter one. Over and over we read, "And God said 'Let there be ... ' and it was so." God was revealing to us how His kind of faith works by showing us how He used His own. He had a desire in His heart, He spoke it with His mouth, and it came to pass just as He desired. It goes like this—believe, say, see.

This is exactly what Jesus was instructing us to do in Mark 11:22–24. Believe it, say it, and we will see it. It is interesting to note that Jesus mentions *saying* three times and *believing* only once. This illustrates the fact that you have to believe one time but you will have to continue to say what you believe until you see the manifestation of it. This is how faith works. Whether we recognize it or not, this is also how we receive everything from God, including salvation. Romans 10:9 told us to confess Jesus as Lord with our mouths, believe in our hearts that God raised Him from the dead, and as a result, salvation manifested in our spirits, and we became new creatures in Christ. We believe, we say, and we receive.

God wanted light on the earth so instead of looking at the darkness and saying what He saw, He spoke what He wanted to see. He believed in His heart and said "Light be" and it was so. Hebrews 11:3 states that *"through faith we understand that the worlds were framed by the word of God, so that things which are seen were not made of things which do appear."* By using His own faith, God framed the worlds using His words, and His invisible Word made the things that are now visible.

What kind of world are your words framing for you? If you have a desire in your heart, believe that it is yours, fill your mouth with God's Word, and speak what you desire. It will come to pass for you. Have a faith-filled day!

Today's Scriptures: Matthew 6:33; Mark 11:22–24; Romans 10:9, Hebrews 11:3.

Today's Prayer/Confession: I will fill my heart with God's Word and believe for those things that align with God's will for my life. From my mouth I dare to say what I believe, and as a result, the things I desire will come to pass in my life!

You Have Been Endowed with the Power to Prosper

My limited knowledge of God was planted in me by my grandmother. She taught me all she knew, and as a result, I loved God, but didn't have a true knowledge of His word. I thought all the blessings mentioned in the Bible belonged to the Jewish people. I knew I wasn't Jewish, so I didn't think I qualified to be blessed on the earth. My blessing was the knowledge that I was going to heaven and I was redeemed from hell. So I grew up thinking that if I ever prospered, it would be by a gracious act of God and not because I qualified for it or deserved it.

Thank God for revelation through the Word of God. I found out that the blessings in the Word of God are for me. I also discovered that it was not solely God's responsibility to make my life prosper. If it were solely God's responsibility, many wouldn't be living on the level they are. There are scores of God-fearing, God-loving, commandment-keeping Christians who are living committed lifestyles, many being faithful in giving their tithe and offerings, yet living at or below the poverty level. God does all things well, and if it was His job and His alone to cause us to prosper, we would all be living in abundance, to the full, with our lives overflowing with His many blessings (John 10:10 Amplified). But we have a part to play.

Proverbs 10:22 states this: *"The blessing of the Lord, **it** maketh rich, and He addeth no sorrow with it."* The word *blessing* comes from the root word *blessed* and it means "to be enabled and endowed with the power to prosper." In Proverbs 10:22, it states that the blessing makes us rich, not God. We understand that it comes from the Lord, but this passage clearly states that the Lord's blessing will increase your life. The word *rich* means "abundantly supplied." When you put this all together it could read like this, "The enablement, the power of the Lord makes us abundantly supplied and God adds no sorrow with that supply."

Another passage to look at is found in Deuteronomy 8:14–18:

> *Then thine heart be lifted up, and thou forget the LORD thy God, which brought thee forth out of the land of Egypt, from the house of bondage ... And thou say in thine heart, 'My power and the might*

of mine hand hath gotten me this wealth.' But thou shalt remember the LORD thy God: for it is he that giveth thee power to get wealth, that he may establish his covenant which he sware unto thy fathers, as it is this day.

Here we see God making it clear that neither our hands nor His bring wealth, but His power does. God supplies **the power** to get wealth, not the wealth itself. Do you know what that power is? It is the same power mentioned in Proverbs 10:22 and known as "The Blessing of the Lord." The blessing is God's super on our natural. It is the enablement to take you from a place of lack to a place of abundance.

It's the heart of God that all believers live on a level that they are able to be blessed, but more importantly for them to be a blessing to others. Our lives are not truly significant until we find ourselves investing in and helping others, and we can't do that if we are not blessed ourselves.

Third John 1:2 is proof that God wants us to prosper, but unless we do something about it, we won't: "*Beloved, I wish above all things that thou MAYEST prosper and be in health, even as thy soul prospereth.*" The words "I wish" and "that thou mayest" are a clear indicator that although every believer has the opportunity, not every believer will take advantage of the opportunity. Will you?

Residing in you right now is God's ability to do more than you could ever dream or imagine, but you must learn how to activate your faith and walk in the fullness of what God has made available to you. The power of God and His blessing is always present and always ready to bring you to a place of overflow. Keep these things at the forefront of your heart and allow the Blessing of the Lord to operate in your life so you can empower someone else.

Have a day full of the manifestation of the Blessing!

Today's Scriptures: John 10:10; Proverbs 10:22; Deuteronomy 8:14–18; 3 John 1:2.

Today's Prayer/Confession: Father, open the eyes of my understanding so I can see all you have given me in this New Covenant. Let your blessings flow in my life as never before because I desire to be a channel of blessing to others. Thank you for giving me the wisdom and understanding to properly handle what you entrust to me, and I will be certain to give you all of the glory for all that will be done. In Jesus's name, Amen!

The Greatest Lesson Learned

Serving God means we have to be willing to give up our own agenda for His. It's not always the easiest thing to do because the flesh wants what it wants. Learning to say "Yes" to God when you really want to say "No" takes a great deal of discipline and trust. I can say "Yes" to Him and walk away from my own will and agenda after I've been assured that He has me and He won't forget about me.

I've lived so much of my life giving to others. From the age of nineteen, I have dedicated my life to serving others. But I vividly remember a time when I stepped out to do something that served my own agenda. It was something I thought would make me great. And I fell flat on my face. Through the years I've learned a lot, but one of the greatest lessons is this: Our lives will never reach the place that God desires if we don't serve others.

Several years ago I was watching an interview with former Governor Arnold Schwarzenegger, and he stated that during a dinner at the home of his wife's parents, he was asked by his late father-in-law, R. Sargent Shriver, "What are you doing to impact someone's life?" Mr. Schwarzenegger proceeded to run down a list of all the movies he had starred in and give an account of all his personal achievements and accomplishments. When he had finished, Shriver said, "Your life isn't worth anything if you aren't using it to help someone else." Sargent Shriver and his wife, Eunice, were the founders of the Special Olympics in 1968 and the creative force behind the Peace Corps in 1961. He knew what he was talking about.

Jesus said it like this in Mark 9:35: *"If any man desire to be first, the same shall be last of all, and servant of all."* Jesus was saying that the way to go up in life is to work from what others would consider the bottom. Greatness is in every one of us, but it's only manifested when we find ourselves investing in the life of another.

Look around you. There are so many people with so many needs and God wants to help them. When you take on the heart of a servant, you help Him do it one life at a time.

Be a blessing today!

Today's Scripture: Mark 9:35.

Today's Confession/Prayer: Father, you gave your Son, and He poured out His life for me and others. Thank you for saving me. Help me to be a reflection of your heart on the earth in serving others. Help me to move with the compassion of Christ in order to bring life, healing, and help to those around me. In Jesus's Name, Amen!

These Bones Can Live

Have you ever gotten to a place in your walk with Christ where you feel as though nothing is moving? Do you feel stumped and in a dry place? You're going to church, still reading your Bible, and praying, but something seems to be missing. When you first gave your heart to Christ, the joy of your salvation was tangible and flowing, but now there almost seems to be emptiness in your heart.

If you've been a Christian for any period of time, you know what I'm talking about. People get to this place, and because of a lack of understanding as to what is truly happening, they come to erroneous conclusions. Some think they've grown beyond their pastor or their church. Some think the Christian life doesn't work for them and choose to live in the flesh, going back to their former way of living. Others go into a place of heaviness and depression. This place is common to all of us, and during times like these, it's important to stay in the Word of God and a place of prayer to press beyond how we feel.

In Psalms 51:12, David is praying a prayer of restoration, asking God to *"restore unto me the joy of my salvation."* The Message Bible says it like this: *"Bring me back from gray exile, put a fresh wind in my sails!"* That's what we need when we find ourselves in spiritually dry places. We need the fresh wind of the Holy Spirit to blow on the sails of our lives.

In Ezekiel 37, God led the prophet Ezekiel to a valley filled with dry bones and asked him a powerful question, "Can these bones live?" He went on to tell Ezekiel to prophesy to the bones. Ezekiel obeyed God and began to prophesy to the entire valley filled with bones. And the nation of Israel was resurrected from a place of dryness and death. God was telling Ezekiel, "You have the power within you to change the fate of an entire nation of people, and that power is in your mouth."

The word *prophesy* in Ezekiel 37:4 is the transliterated Hebrew word *"naba,"* which means "to speak under the divine influence." When Ezekiel spoke to the dry bones, his words were divinely infused with the power of God, and as a result, his words brought life and restoration.

Proverbs 18:21 states that death and life are in the power of your tongue, and if you have the power of God living in you, you can use that power to restore life to your own place of dryness. Sometimes you may need someone else to help "jump start" you, but make sure you get what you need. If you don't feel like you can spiritually feed yourself, put on a CD of someone else teaching a biblically sound message or listen to the Bible on CD and spend time praying.

The greatest way to refuel spiritually is found in Ephesians 5:14–20:

Wherefore he saith, Awake thou that sleepest, and arise from the dead, and Christ shall give thee light. See then that ye walk circumspectly, not as fools, but as wise, Redeeming the time, because the days are evil. Wherefore be ye not unwise, but understanding what the will of the Lord is. And be not drunk with wine, wherein is excess; but be filled with the Spirit; Speaking to yourselves in psalms and hymns and spiritual songs, singing and making melody in your heart to the Lord; Giving thanks always for all things unto God and the Father in the name of our Lord Jesus Christ.

In this passage, Paul is giving us the way to be "awakened" spiritually. It comes first by not being drunk with wine (or any other substance), but being filled with the Spirit. How? By speaking and singing to yourself and doing so under the divine influence of the Spirit.

When you find yourself in a place of dryness, do what Ezekiel did. Use God's Word and prophesy to the dry places in your life. Ephesians 5 makes it even clearer: *"Be filled with the Spirit; speaking to yourselves ..."* This is how we come from a place of spiritual lethargy to a place of renewed strength and joy. When we take the time to prophesy to ourselves, we will see the life of God flowing in our lives once again!

Speak to yourself today!

Today's Scriptures: Psalms 51:12; Ezekiel 37; Proverbs 18:21; Ephesians 5:14–20.

Today's Prayer/Confession: When I am in a dry place, I will use the Word of God to speak to my life. I won't say what I feel or what I see. I will only say what I believe to be true based on the Word of God, and it will come to pass in my life!

Love the One You're With

Many years ago, singer-songwriter Stephen Stills wrote a song called "Love the One You're With." Although I may not agree with all the lyrics in the song, the title is meaningful. I was thinking this morning about my husband and children and all that comes with being in their lives. Using Ebonics … It ain't always easy. But there is something deep in my heart that embraces all that comes with my family. I've learned to accept their personalities, shortcomings, and highs and lows, and love them all individually. I don't expect one to act like the other, and though I'm often tempted, I will not allow myself to measure one against the other. I accept them all just the way they are. I do my best to instill the wisdom of God, based on the Word of God, in their lives because it's my responsibility and their spiritual heritage.

Accepting everyone is not an easy thing to do, especially when they make decisions that are totally contrary to what has been invested in their lives. In those times we have to learn to fight to love the one we are with. I've experienced so many disappointing things, but the love of God has helped me endure them all. I can't say I haven't cried, isolated myself, or desired to leave, because I have. However, during those times, God's voice always comes to me, reminding me of His love for me.

When I measure the level of God's love in my own life—the many times He has forgiven me when I disappointed Him—I can't seem to find it in myself to hold grudges with others for very long. Yes, I've gotten angry. Yes, I've thrown a fit or two. But I cannot live in that place because I was loved, forgiven, and embraced when I was, as Paul put it, "a chief sinner" myself (1 Timothy 1:15).

What I'm trying to say is that God has given us the individuals in our families for a specific purpose—the good, the bad, and the ugly. Each one plays a part in God's plan, and not one is a mistake. I don't care how they got here or how it came to be that they are a part of your life. Ultimately, God knew they were coming, He knew they would rub you the wrong way, and He sent them into your life anyway. Doesn't that just make you want to throw your hands in the air and give Him praise? Okay, maybe not.

You are a believer and the light in you is strong enough to draw your family to Christ. Jesus said in John 13:35 that *all* men will know you are

His disciples by the love you have for one another. The greatest witness for Christ is not in your ability to preach at your family or your isolation from those who may not be like you, but rather your ability to love them in spite of who they are or what their lifestyles may be like.

When you walk in the love of Christ toward your family, you are lifting Christ up, and although John 12:32 was symbolic of Christ being raised up on the cross, it still holds true in other areas. When Christ is lifted up, He draws men to himself. Let the love of God in you be released toward your family. Start with the one who seems to be the least embracing of who you are in their life. Pray for them and then listen for the Holy Spirit to show you ways to subtly knock down the walls that stand between you.

In 1 Corinthians 13, we are told, "Love Never Fails," so it won't fail you when you have made the decision to love the one you're with. God bless you today!

Today's Scriptures: 1 Timothy 1:15; John 13:35; John 12:32; 1 Corinthians 13.

Today's Prayer/Confession: Father, loving my family isn't always easy, but Romans 5:5 says that You put your love in my heart so I can love my family as You desire. Help me to forgive quickly, and teach me how to embrace them when I feel hurt and disappointed. I want to love them the way that You have continually loved me. In Jesus's Name, Amen!

Your Harvest in Life

"Don't be under any illusion: you cannot make a fool of God! A man's harvest in life will depend entirely on what he sows." This is the JB Phillips Translation of Galatians 6:7. I could stop writing here. "A man's harvest in life will depend *entirely* on what he sows." *Really?* Do you know what the word *entirely* means? It means "solely, totally, exclusively and completely." I want you to look at your life right now. If this scripture is true, everything you see is a result of what you have been sowing. (Don't stop reading here.)

Whether we realize it or not, once we get to the stage in life where our parents no longer have governing authority over us, we become accountable for all that is sown or planted in our lives. There are three types of seeds: word seeds, action seeds, and thought seeds. So your harvest in life will come from one of these three areas.

This was a difficult reality for me, because when examining my own life, I recognized that I had planted many wrong "word seeds" and could clearly see the harvest. In some cases, the harvest field was so great that the only option was to set a blazing fire to it. If you want to know the truth, that's actually how it got that way in the first place.

And the tongue is a fire, a world of iniquity: so is the tongue among our members, that it defileth the whole body, and setteth on fire the course of nature; and it is set on fire of hell. (James 3:6)

The Message Bible says it like this: *"It only takes a spark, remember, to set off a forest fire. A careless or wrongly placed word out of your mouth can do that. By our speech we can ruin the world, turn harmony to chaos, throw mud on a reputation, send the whole world up in smoke, and go up in smoke with it, smoke right from the pit of hell."*

The words of our mouths are laying the stones of our lives. What we say about something is what we sow, and our harvest will be a result of our own words.

When my daughter Kayla was around two, I began to notice the strength of her will. Because she was so young, I attributed it to her age and repeatedly told my husband, "No, she doesn't need to be disciplined. She'll be okay. She will grow out of it." As she got older, my conversation went from "She'll be okay" to "Honey, she is something else!" I knew the power of my words, but I didn't realize that I was calling her a "something else." I didn't know what a "something else" was. I was trying to watch my words, but my heart was speaking loud and clear. "Something else" was another way of saying "stubborn and rebellious." "Something else" *is* something else, and you'd better believe me and find another selection of words.

Many years later, I am working overtime using my words to turn "something else" into "someone else"! I have victory in Jesus without a doubt, but the seed of my words is now the harvest of my reality. I have to use the Word of God to uproot the former harvest while at the same time sowing good word seeds that will produce a good harvest we can enjoy. I want my words to be a springboard into a life of blessing my daughter will benefit from when she takes on the responsibility of sowing seeds for herself.

If you can look at your life and see a harvest that isn't quite what you wanted, it's never too late to turn the course of things. Start today! Use your thoughts, words, and actions to plant seeds today that will bring a welcomed harvest tomorrow. Everything you do today is a stone for your tomorrow. Live with the understanding that you are sowing seeds all day long. Ask yourself, "Do I want what I am releasing today coming back on me in my future?" If the answer is "no," don't sow the seed.

God bless you today!

Today's Scriptures: Galatians 6:7; James 3:6.

Today's Prayer/Confession: I will sow seeds of blessing in my life. Father, help me to understand what I'm saying, doing, and thinking before it is released from me. Allow me to sow seeds of mercy and grace to the hearer and actions of blessing to the receiver. I love and appreciate you for revealing this truth to my heart. In Jesus's name, Amen!

Don't Let Lethargy Steal from You

One morning I woke very early and heard the word *lethargy*. I had heard it before, but for some reason couldn't remember its meaning. This was in my pre-Internet days, so I pulled out the dictionary and found that lethargy is defined as "the quality or state of being drowsy and dull, listless and unenergetic; indifferent and lazy; apathetic or sluggish inactivity."

There are over ten thousand promises in the Word of God, but every promise must be received and/or taken in order to walk in the fullness of it. Many people want God's blessings; they really want everything He has promised, but for one reason or another they just don't seem to experience them.

When I was younger we used to play a game called tug-of-war. It was a contest of strength in which two teams tug on opposite ends of a rope, each trying to pull the other across a dividing line. Sometimes I would pull with all my might because I wanted to win. Other times I may have found myself against a family member I didn't want to beat, so I would hold the rope in a listless, lazy way. I wouldn't always give my strength to help my team win.

This is what happens in our spiritual lives. Everything God has provided for us is ours for the taking—if we choose to take it. A lethargic hand will not pull or place a demand on the things God has for it. Matthew 11:12 (NKJV) states: "*The Kingdom of heaven suffers violence and the violent take it by force.*" The word *violence* is translated as "pressure," and the word *violent* is "strong and forceful." In order for you to walk in the blessings of God, you will have to become strong and forceful, using the pressure of God's Word.

The blessings are for you, and they are waiting for you to receive them, but you won't receive them if you allow a spirit of lethargy to overtake you. You have to pull with all your might to lay hold of everything you need to receive to be a blessing on the earth. Too many Christians live without taking advantage of all God has provided in the Kingdom, and there are so many blessings just waiting for you and me!

I can't confirm this, but I once heard the story of a man who had the experience of going to heaven when he was a six-year-old boy. One of the most powerful revelations came when he shared that Jesus had been giving him a tour of heaven when they walked into what looked like a warehouse. The boy was shocked to see so many blessings, including parts of the physical body, such as eyes of various colors, vital organs, and limbs. The little boy opened his mouth to ask Jesus, "What is this place?" And before he could get the words out of his mouth, Jesus replied, "This is the storehouse of unclaimed blessings." I absolutely lost it. The thought that there is an entire storehouse in heaven with blessings that many, including me, have failed to claim overwhelms me.

Even if that storehouse doesn't exist, we know that the realm of faith does, and in it, waiting for us, is all that God has promised. So don't allow lethargy to steal from you any longer. Use your strength. Pull on the rope of the promises of God, and let's clean out the storehouse of unclaimed blessings!

God bless you today!

Today's Scriptures: Matthew 11:12; Mark 11:22–24; Hebrews 11.

Today's Prayer/Confession: Father, in the name of Jesus, help me to recognize any area of my life where there is lethargy. I am strong in you and in the power of your might, and I will lay hold of every blessing that you have in "store" for me. I receive your promises, and I position myself to be a channel of blessing for someone else. Amen!

Love You with My Life

Jesus, here I pray; on my knees before you
I live for you today; Because I do adore you
I will not be afraid; Only watch and pray
To see your glad return

I'll put my trust in you; 'Til my life is completed
Do all as unto you; Believing all you've stated
I work to live in peace; In spite of tribulation
Until you come again

Please know that I love you; I'll stay by your side
Worship you in spirit; Dear Lord, be my guide
I will not suffer long; For you have suffered for me
I love you with my life, love you with my life,
Love you with my life.

This song was written by Bryan Duncan in 1985. I loved it then, and I still love it today. Loving God with your life means you are willing to lay aside anything and everything to please Him. It is doing so when it's easy and when it's painful. It is giving yourself to Him totally and completely, leaving your life open to Him. Nothing is held back, nothing is untouchable, and nothing is unreasonable. No relationship, job, habit, tradition, or mindset is off limits. He gets right of entry to all of it.

If you have been struggling to embrace or let go of something in your life, and deep in your heart of hearts you know God has been dealing with you about it, submit to Him. Don't continue to avoid the issue. Give yourself over to Him. Whether you can see it or not, it really is going to benefit you in the end. Everything God has for you is to better your life. There is nothing He will require of you that is designed to destroy or deplete you. It will always increase and build you in some way. His plan is always the best for your life.

"For I know the thoughts that I think toward you, saith the LORD, thoughts of peace, and not of evil, to give you an expected end" (Jeremiah 29:11).

"'I know the plans I have for you,' announces the Lord. 'I want you to enjoy success. I do not plan to harm you. I will give you hope for the years to come'" (Jeremiah 29:11 NIRV).

Today's Scripture: Jeremiah 29:11.

Today's Prayer/Confession: Father, everything I have in life I offer to you, my heart, my mind, and my direction. Help me in those areas I haven't totally given to you. I want what you want for me. I want to love you with my life by obeying you and submitting my will to you. You said you have an expected end for me, and I am determined that I will reach your predetermined place for my life, in Jesus's name, Amen.

You Are an Heir

One day I was goofing around online and I Googled the word *unclaimed*. I was amazed to see so many sites for unclaimed money and property. I clicked on one and was shocked to see an exhaustive list of names of people who had money just waiting to be claimed. I'm not sure where all the money came from, but I'm confident, because of the amounts, that a great portion was from inheritances, and unfortunately, those individuals don't know they are heirs.

An heir is an individual who inherits the rights to the property and possessions of a deceased person. That's the definition from dictionary. com. But the interlinear Greek gives this definition: One who receives his allotted possession by right of son-ship. That blesses me!

When you accepted Christ into your life, according to Galatians 4:6, God sent the spirit of His Son into your heart. When He did, your heart recognized and received God as Father, and from that moment you could cry out to Him as "Abba," or "dear Father," because the reality of the relationship was established. This is *not* the spirit of an adopted son, but the spirit of *the Son*.

God is no longer a being in heaven with whom we have no relationship. He literally became your Heavenly Father, so you now have son-ship privileges just like His other Son, Christ Jesus. You have access to all the Father possesses, just as you would with a good natural father. When Jesus died on the cross, His death made you an heir of Father God and a joint heir with Christ. Remember, you don't become an heir until someone dies.

"And because ye are sons, God hath sent forth the Spirit of his Son into your hearts, crying, Abba, Father. Wherefore thou art no more a servant, but a son; and if a son, then an heir of God through Christ" (Galatians 4:6–7).

"And if children, then heirs; heirs of God, and joint-heirs with Christ; if so be that we suffer with him, that we may be also glorified together" (Romans 8:17).

Choose to live your life inheriting all the blessings God has for you, and as you do, you position yourself to bless others. Jesus paid a great price so you could become an heir of God. As a son, don't let your name get on the list of individuals who haven't claimed what is rightfully theirs. Get busy inheriting the promises as told in Hebrews 6:12. Are you an heir? Will you claim your inheritance? I believe you will. Go for it!

Bless you today!

Today's Scriptures: Galatians 4:6–7; Romans 8:17; Hebrews 6:12.

Today's Prayer/Confession: Father, open my eyes so I can come to know all you have given me through the death, burial, and resurrection of Jesus Christ. I desire to live as you have positioned me, but more importantly, I desire to be a channel of blessing to others. Thank you for your Word and your wisdom that reveals who I am and what I have. In Jesus's name I pray, Amen!

Faith in the Heart/Doubt in the Head

Is it possible to have faith in your heart and doubt in your head? I'll answer the question with a question. Is it possible to be born again in your spirit and still have a mind that isn't transformed? The answer on both accounts is "yes."

In the ninth chapter of Mark, you can read the account of the man who brought his son to the disciples to cast out an evil spirit. The evil spirit would cause the boy to have seizures so intense the child would fall to the ground foaming at the mouth. The evil spirit tried several times to make the boy commit suicide by throwing himself into a fire or the river. The disciples couldn't help, so the father went to Jesus. Here is their discourse:

> *Jesus replied ... , "Bring the boy to me." So they brought him. When the spirit saw Jesus, it immediately threw the boy into a convulsion. He fell to the ground and rolled around, foaming at the mouth. Jesus asked the boy's father, "How long has he been like this?" "From childhood," he answered. "It has often thrown him into fire or water to kill him. But if you can do anything, take pity on us and help us." "If you can'?" said Jesus. "Everything is possible for him who believes." Immediately the boy's father exclaimed, **"I do believe; help me overcome my unbelief!"** (Mark 9:19–24 NIV)*

It's interesting to note the words of this precious father in verse 24, "I do believe; help me overcome my unbelief!" It seems like a contradiction. Either he believed or he didn't. I would venture to say he had faith in his heart but doubt in his head. His heart embraced the fact that Jesus had the ABILITY to heal his son, but his mind wasn't certain that He WOULD, so it produced doubt and unbelief. In verse 23, Jesus had to reassure him that He was not just *able*, but He was also *willing* to heal the child, provided the father could believe it. The father cried out to Jesus to help him overcome his unbelief and the boy was healed.

Does this sound like a personal struggle you have ever had? Were there times when you knew God could do something? Your heart was strong and fixed on the fact that He could, but the challenge came with the idea that He would. Like the boy's father, you had faith in your heart but there was doubt in your head because you were unsure.

Assurance comes when we know the will of God. Faith begins where the will of God is known! We must learn to be like the man in Mark 9 and cry out to Jesus, who is the Word of God. We have to take the time to feed on God's Word so our mind lines up with the truth in our heart. The goal is to get them both to agree with the Word of God.

One of the greatest ways to get your mind and heart connected is to speak out loud what you believe in your heart. Matthew 12:34 says: "*Out of the abundance of the heart the mouth speaketh.*" The NIV says, "*Out of the overflow of the heart the mouth speaks.*" Whether we realize it or not, the mind respects the mouth.

If you've ever noticed when you are thinking about something and you open your mouth to speak, the mind stops thinking to hear what your mouth has to say. Here's a little exercise to prove it. Count to ten and right in the middle of counting say the word "cheeseburger." When you say "cheeseburger," your mind will stop counting to hear what your mouth has to say. The words of your mouth interrupt the thoughts in your mind. This is why it is so important to fill your mouth with the Word of God.

The Lord told this to Joshua in Joshua 1:8 (NKJV): "*This book of the law shall not depart from your mouth but you are to meditate on it day and night.*" God knew that if Joshua kept the Word in his mouth, he would keep the Word on his mind. Having the Word on your mind is the first step to having it deeply rooted in your heart. In the end, you are aligning every part of your being with God's Word. You use your mouth to speak the Word (body), your mind to meditate on the Word (soul), and your heart to embrace the Word (spirit). (See 1 Thessalonians 5:23.) When you do this, you will know with assurance and certainty that when you call on Jesus, you will have the petition that you desire of Him.

Today's Scriptures: Mark 9:19–24; Matthew 12:34; Joshua 1:8; 1 Thessalonians 5:23.

Today's Prayer/Confession: Today I will align my mind, body, and heart with God's Word. Every area of doubt will be removed as I speak and meditate on God's Word. I am victorious in every situation, and there is no weapon formed against me that will prosper, because I walk in the knowledge of God's Word!

Check Your Pride, Balance Your Life

In the late 1980s, I was driving down the street in my little Isuzu when the most beautiful car went zooming by. I didn't know what type of car it was, but later discovered it was a BMW. And was it nice! Although I wanted one, I couldn't afford a car like that at the time. I was not only a single mother of twins, but I was also going to school and working a full-time job. So I decided to use my faith. After standing in faith for almost three years, I finally got my BMW. It was a beautiful 5 Series. I did my homework long before I got it. I knew the ins and outs of "The Ultimate Driving Machine."

I'll never forget the feeling that came over me the day I sat in that car. I was proud to be the official owner of a "Beamer" in both the good way ... and the bad. The thrill of using my faith and seeing the manifestation of my prayer boosted my faith to an all-time high. At the same time, the attention it brought to me personally sent my pride soaring right along with my faith. I started driving more slowly through the church parking lot, making sure I was seen in my new set of wheels. And when I drove to work, I would park in the front row, right in front of the door.

"Practically everything that goes on in the world - wanting your own way, wanting everything for yourself, wanting to appear important - has nothing to do with the Father. It just isolates you from him" (1 John 2:16 Message).

Pride is a creepy little thing. It springs up in the most unsuspecting places, and when it does, if it is not dealt with according to the Word of God, it will contaminate our motives and position us for a great big fall. *"First pride, then the crash—the bigger the ego, the harder the fall"* (Proverbs 16:18 Message).

When our motives are rooted in pride, it is nothing more than a manifestation of the flesh. 1 Peter 1:24 states: *"All flesh is as grass."* In other words, it needs to be cut down. Whenever we find ourselves obeying the desires of the flesh, it will isolate us from the Father. 1 Peter 5:5 says, *"God resists the proud."* Pride is like an insect repellent. Repellents have a substance bugs cannot tolerate. The two can't intermingle. When a bug comes in contact with that substance, it drives them away. Pride operates in exactly the same fashion. It is the repellant that keeps God away from your life, and the substance in pride is the flesh. God and the flesh can never and will never intermingle.

One day a check-and-balance moment came for me. I was driving to work praying in my BMW, thanking God for being so good, and the word of the Lord came to me strongly saying, "Park the car a block away from the office." Huh? "Park the car a block away from the office." I knew it was God. Neither the devil nor my flesh would have said it. They wanted me on the front row with everybody watching as I stepped out. I drove right past the parking lot and parked my car one block away from the building just as God said and walked to the office.

What was God doing? He was helping me crucify my flesh. I parked my car away from the building for a solid year because that's how long it took my flesh to come into subjection. I did not park in the lot again until I could do so without thinking about who was seeing me.

Crucifying the flesh and operating with pure motives is not the easiest thing to do, but thank God we have the Holy Spirit living inside of us leading and guiding us into the truth. God loves us too much to allow us to live in a way that would keep Him away from our lives. Don't let pride have any place in you.

Have a great day!

Today's Scriptures: 1 John 2:16; Proverbs 16:18; 1 Peter 1:24; 1 Peter 5:5.

Today's Prayer/Confession: Father, thank you for the ability to crucify my flesh through the work of the Holy Spirit within me. I am not subject to my flesh, but my spirit, and I thank you that I have the power to overcome the weakness of my flesh. Pride has no place in me! In Jesus's name, Amen!

Release the Power

I've often been asked the question, "Why don't we see the types of miracles in our day that they saw in the days of Jesus and the apostles?" The question used to stump me because I didn't have an answer. It's clear that Jesus's earthly ministry consisted of three things: preaching, teaching, and healing. It's also clear that the disciples continued to operate in the same pattern of ministry after Jesus ascended to heaven to be with the Father. Throughout the book of Acts, you see the manifestation of the power of God through the followers of Jesus. Blinded eyes were opened, people were delivered from bondage, and the lame walked. All of this took place at the official launch of the Church.

When we became Christians, we became a part of the exact same body of believers. We are the Church! So what happened? Where did the power go? Why don't we see the miracles? Why aren't the blinded eyes being opened? Why isn't the deaf man being healed? Why aren't the lame walking? Why don't we see people being delivered from satanic oppression?

> *And these signs shall follow them that believe; In my name shall they cast out devils; they shall speak with new tongues; They shall take up serpents; and if they drink any deadly thing, it shall not hurt them; they shall lay hands on the sick, and they shall recover. (Mark 16:17–18)*

My husband and I were conducting a service at our local church when suddenly I had an inspiration to lay hands on people for healing. When we began, I felt like I was laying empty hands on empty heads. There seemed to be no anointing whatsoever, and I'm not one to do something just because it might be a good idea. I was certain I was obeying God, but nothing seemed to be happening. When I arrived home, I continued to ponder what had taken place when up came these words: "When you lay hands on people, it takes faith to release the healing anointing from within you. (These signs shall follow them that *believe*.) The anointing must be activated, so continue to lay your hands on the sick even though you may not see anything happen immediately. Faith is working. Give your spirit time to learn how to release the virtue of my power from within and you will see results."

If you study Mark 5:30, Luke 6:19 and Luke 8:46, you will see Jesus laying hands on people or people laying hands on Him, and when they did, power flowed out of His spirit. The King James Bible calls it *virtue*, which is defined in the Greek as "the power to perform miracles." That is what the world needs, the power of God performing miracles in their lives. I once heard someone say, "Healing is the dinner bell." When the Body of Christ begins to function as it was created to, we will see people running to Christ and lives dramatically changed. God hasn't lost His recipe for healing. He still knows how to open blind eyes. He still knows how to make the lame walk and the deaf hear. He knows, but we have a part to play.

The sixteenth chapter of Mark says believers will lay hands on the sick and they *shall* recover. The word *shall* comes from the original Greek word "*Echo*" which means "to have, to hold, to possess in the mind." So when we lay our hands on the sick, they will have and hold health. Do you know someone who could use your help holding on to their health? I certainly do, and it's powerful to think that the power of God to heal can flow through me if I believe. So what are you going to do? Act on the Word of God. Start in your household. Release the virtue or power in your spirit to bring health and healing to your children, spouse, or loved ones. Get the power flowing from within, and let's bring the power present in the ministry of Jesus and the early Church back to the forefront!

Have an awesome Day!

Today's Scriptures: The Book of Acts; Mark 16:17–18; Mark 5:30; Luke 6:19; Luke 8:46.

Today's Prayer/Confession: Father, today I will release your power in order to bring recovery to someone else's life. Let your power flow through me as it did in the days of the early church and in the ministry days of Jesus.

Discouragement Has No Place in Me

Sometimes I think about all the people I have helped or influenced in some way. Most of my life, I have given my all to advance another's purpose, doing everything in the background. I never pushed my way to the forefront to be seen or recognized. All I wanted was to get under their mission and help bring God's purpose for their lives to pass. It's a blessing to watch God use the fruits of your labor to move another forward.

There were times, however, when I found myself feeling heavy because it seemed as though things were happening for those I'd helped, but very little was happening for me. I've also had to fight the temptation to fear that if I did step out, the doors wouldn't open for me as they have others. These thoughts brought an overwhelming sense of sadness. I didn't want to give myself over to them, but one thing was certain: Discouragement, a mild form of depression, was trying to settle in.

Discouragement is not exclusive. If you walk with Christ for any significant period of time, you will have opportunities to be discouraged. Its definition is similar to depression, which is "a sunken place or part, an area lower than the surrounding surface." Depression is the feeling of sadness, gloom, or dejection, and discouragement feels the same. The important thing is not to allow the spirit of discouragement to lock its hold on you, because it can be difficult to shake off once it does.

Discouragement is not limited to those who live a bad life. You can be doing your absolute best and it will creep up on you. It's no respecter of persons. Great men of the Bible had days of discouragement, including Jesus. The focus should not be the fact that discouragement has come. It should be on what we do when it comes. Jesus prayed. He didn't lock himself in a room isolated from others. He didn't overeat or under-eat, go shopping, or use drugs or alcohol. He didn't stay in bed, take sleeping pills, or spend endless days crying. He prayed!

You and I can handle depression exactly as Jesus did. We have to move ourselves into prayer, knowing God can be trusted to take care of us. Depression is not your friend, and it can have no place in your life; don't embrace it, instead know that God will not forget about you. Hebrews 6:10 (NLT) says this: "*For God is not unjust. He will not forget how hard you have worked for him and how you have shown your love to him by caring for other believers, as you still do."* He won't forget about you. Your day is coming. You stand firm. Keep your head up, and know that God's got your back!

Have a great day!

Today's Scriptures: Hebrews 6:10; Proverbs 3:5.

Today's Prayer/Confession: Discouragement has no place in my life. I will trust in the Lord with all my heart and lean not unto my own understanding. I will pray when my heart becomes overwhelmed, knowing that God can be trusted with my life!

Consistency is the Key

Have you ever met someone who is the same all the time? No matter what the circumstance, this person's personality remains the same. My husband is that way. He is one of the most consistent individuals I know. Even if he gets upset, there is consistency in his pattern of behavior. His commitment to me never changes. I remember times when I would "cut up" and thought for sure he was going to shut down on me. Surprisingly, he woke the next morning with the exact same words as always: "Good morning, beautiful."

I would be thinking, *Good morning, beautiful? Shouldn't he be packing his clothes to leave?* Not when you live by the spiritual force called "consistency."

Consistency is the ability to hold together and retain your form or firmness. It's being the same no matter what may be happening around you. When you are consistent, you are committed, and your commitment doesn't change with the circumstances. A lack of consistency is why so many relationships have gone bad or ended. People just don't want to go the distance when it gets rough. As pastors, my husband and I have witnessed and experienced firsthand the division inconsistency brings into relationships. We have seen how it impacts children, marriages, and ministries. People are with you until times get tough, and when times get tough, the inconsistent get going.

In Acts 12:25, we read the account of the mission ministry of Paul and Barnabas. A man named John Mark was taken into the ministry with them, but in chapter 13, after some tough times, he went back to Jerusalem, completely abandoning the ministry. If you read further, Barnabas wanted Mark to rejoin the group, but Paul felt Mark wasn't profitable because he had abandoned them previously. The dispute about Mark became so intense that it split the ministry of Paul and Barnabas. Unfortunately, after this dispute, nothing further is mentioned of the ministry of Barnabas. Years later, as recounted in 2 Timothy 4:11, Paul told Timothy to bring Mark to him because he had become profitable for the ministry. Mark became profitable when he developed a life of consistency.

We want profitable relationships. God wants them to be strong and lasting, but consistency is a major key. We don't want to be disqualified in life from the places of blessing that God has for us.

"*Therefore, my beloved brethren, be ye steadfast, unmovable, always abounding in the work of the Lord, forasmuch as ye know that your labour is not in vain in the Lord*" (1 Corinthians 15:58).

The Message Bible says it this way: "*With all this going for us, my dear, dear friends, stand your ground. And don't hold back. Throw yourselves into the work of the Master, confident that nothing you do for him is a waste of time or effort.*"

Stand your ground, my friend. Don't allow the circumstances of life to toss you around. Keep your footing and God will reward your consistency.

Have a great day!

Today's Scriptures: Acts 12:25; Acts 13; Acts 15; 2 Timothy 4:11; 1 Corinthians 15:58.

Today's Prayer/Confession: Father, today I will live my life based on the Word of God and not on the circumstances surrounding me. I thank you for the strength you give to stand firm in truth and not be given over to the swaying of emotions. In Jesus's name, Amen!

Obedience

When I have to discipline my children, there are times when I see this strange expression, almost a smirk, come across their faces; it seems to say, "Okay, she's worked herself up! Winding up for the pitch! Here it comes! … almost there! … out of the park! … the 'O' word!"

I'll stand there infuriated sometimes, thinking to myself, *Don't you look at me with that sarcastic tone of voice!* It's almost as though I can hear their thoughts. My kids are constantly hearing the speech about obedience. Why? Because I understand that obedience is the catalyst to a life of blessing.

Obedience is following God's instructions. It is willingly and submissively complying with what He tells you to do and doing so with the right heart and attitude. Whenever you have been instructed by the Lord to do a particular thing, you will find that your flesh will immediately want to do the opposite. That's the nature of our flesh. It always opposes God (Galatians 5).

For example, in 1 Thessalonians 4:3, God instructs us not to engage in sexual activity before marriage, and because God said it, the flesh wants it—because the flesh always opposes God. If you look at 1 Corinthians 7:3–6, God instructs married people not to "withhold" sex from one another. But because God said it, after people get married, one of the major problems in their marriage is having a desire to connect sexually. Why? Again, because the flesh opposes God, it is not willing to submit or comply with His ways or His word. As a result, we often find ourselves struggling with obedience.

Paul said something like this: "I want to do right, but evil is always present with me. I'm willing to do it, but there is another force working in my members causing me to go in the opposite direction." I paraphrased Romans 7:21, but you get the picture. Paul was saying, "My heart wants to obey, but my flesh wants what it wants." Jesus said it like this in Matthew 26:41: *"The spirit indeed is willing, but the flesh is weak."* So what can we do? How do we position ourselves for God's blessings through obedience if we have this constant fight going on?

The most important thing is crucifying the flesh. Your flesh will team up with the devil and have you doing things totally opposite of God's will.

Crucifying the flesh means you have to discipline yourself—saying "no" and then sticking to it, regardless of the pressure. Whenever you set out to obey the voice of God, there is going to be another voice that comes to tempt you to disobey. That is what happened in the Garden of Eden. God spoke and Adam and Eve set out to obey, but the voice of the serpent came and they listened to him instead of God. Adam and Eve would have continued to enjoy the blessings of the garden had they obeyed God's voice.

The same holds true for you and me. God speaks to us, and immediately the mind of the flesh, fueled by the enemy, raises its deceptive voice, and we find ourselves in a place of decision. Who you listen to is going to determine where you go from there. You're either going to obey God, or you're going to obey the enemy of God. It's always your choice. If you choose God, you'll remain in the Garden. If you choose the flesh, like Adam did, you'll be kicked out of the blessing of God to work by the sweat of your brow.

Don't listen to your carnal, fleshly mind. Don't go after what feels good or what's easy and convenient. Go toward the direction given by God. Thoughts of misdirection are going to come, but you don't have to submit to them or follow them. Never forget this: You can't stop a bird from flying over your head, but you can stop him from building a nest in it. You can't stop Satan from bringing thoughts to your mind, but you can stop him from building his castle in it. Don't let the enemy build a nest of misguided, misdirected thoughts in your mind. Choose to obey God! Remember He said that you will live if you do.

"I call heaven and earth to record this day against you, that I have set before you life and death, blessing and cursing: therefore choose life, that both thou and thy seed may live" (Deuteronomy 30:19).

Have an obedient day!

Today's Scriptures: Galatians 5; 1 Thessalonians 4:3; 1 Corinthians 7:3–6; Romans 7:21; Matthew 26:41; Deuteronomy 30:19.

Today's Prayer/Confession: Father, today I obey your voice. I respond when you speak to me and ask for sensitivity to your voice. You said in your Word that the voice of the stranger I would not follow. Thank you for the Holy Spirit who lives and abides in me. Thank you that He will lead me into all that is true. In Jesus's name, Amen!

In His Presence

This morning I awakened earlier than usual with a very strong pull on my heart to come before God. I thought about the days in my early teens when I rode the bus home from school, and the entire way home I would gaze out the window, mumbling under my breath words of love and admiration to God. Some days, my heart would get so full of Him that once my bus stop came, I would run to the house and literally collapse to my knees on the floor. I didn't have all the eloquent words or know the etiquette of prayer. I just loved Him and wanted to spend my time in fellowship, communing in His presence. I imagine this was the case with Mary when she was supposed to be helping her sister, Martha, but instead she was found sitting at the feet of Jesus.

Our lives are too busy. There's too much going on—too much movement and too many decisions being made that were never prayed out or prayed through in the presence of God. The Father wants times of stillness in our lives, times of sitting, kneeling, and waiting because He has something He wants to say. These are the days to have your ear to His heart. Listen. Listen for His wisdom and instructions. Position yourself to hear and receive. He's all-knowing and has all of the answers you need. Learn to quiet your mind and your heart.

When you position yourself in the presence of God, His love overwhelms you, and you grow in your knowledge of Him. I love the Amplified translation of Ephesians 3:19:

[That you may really come] to know [practically, through experience for yourselves] the love of Christ, which far surpasses mere knowledge [without experience]; that you may be filled [through all your being] unto all the fullness of God [may have the richest measure of the divine Presence, and become a body wholly filled and flooded with God Himself]!

The thought that I could have the richest measure of God's divine presence and a life wholly filled and flooded with God Himself blesses me. When I read this, I determined that if it was possible, I would live my life in pursuit of it; because it is written, I know with certainty that it is possible, and it's mine for the taking.

But it doesn't come without a price. We must find ourselves in the continual pursuit of the presence of God. It's not that He's running away from us and we are chasing after Him, but rather we are making a daily decision to enter into His presence that is available to us through the shed blood of Jesus Christ. It's going after what is rightfully ours with all that is in us.

Continual feeding on the Word of God and spending time before Him in prayer is essential. Moses was an example of a man whose life was filled with God. In Exodus we can see that he spent an enormous amount of time in the presence of God, and as a result, his face began to shine. Even though he didn't recognize it, the people saw it. Moses never had to say, "I spent three hours in prayer today." Prayer was his lifestyle, and although he never advertised it, God's presence so inundated his life that Moses couldn't contain it. God was literally seeping through Moses.

Oh, how we should long for this! I picture our lives much like sponges filled with water, and when people have a need, all they have to do is touch the sponge of their lives, and God Himself will seep out, providing all they need.

It was the premise that you would be in the presence of God that moved Jesus to say, *"Let your light so shine, that men may see your good works and glorify your Father which is in heaven"* (Matthew 5:16). The "good works" include the time that you have spent in His presence, filling yourself of all that He is. So let it shine, let it shine, let it shine!

God bless you today!

Today's Scriptures: Ephesians 3:19; Matthew 5:16.

Today's Prayer/Confession: Father, today I lift my life to you. I long to be in your presence, and I allow you to speak to my heart. All I desire to be is found in you, and I ask you to fill me with a deeper desire to fellowship with you. In Jesus's name, Amen!

Love Yourself!

"'And you must love the LORD your God with all your heart, all your soul, all your mind, and all your strength.' The second is equally important: 'Love your neighbor as yourself.' No other commandment is greater than these" (Mark 12:30–31 NLT).

I got the first part, but the second? Love your neighbor as you do yourself? Hmmm ... do you love yourself? Maybe the reason we struggle to love other people is because we struggle to genuinely love ourselves. I find that people who have made mistakes in life can't love themselves enough to accept what Christ did on the cross, embracing His forgiveness. These same individuals often have problems forgiving others. Forgiveness is an act of love.

Jesus said that all of the Ten Commandments were summed up in the two I quoted above. So that means if you love yourself, you're not going to steal, kill, covet, or commit adultery, because those things don't just violate God's law, they hurt you and open the door for Satan to gain access to your life.

Love yourself enough to take the time to think about what hurting someone else is going to cost you. Get a good mental picture, and chances are you will never want to reach the point of hurting someone else. It's easier to love your neighbor when you understand that your actions are going to hurt you. Whenever I have slowed down and prayerfully considered things, I have not moved beyond my thoughts. My thinking things through gave God time to reveal what the consequences would be for me, and in the end I decided not to do it.

You can't think selfishly when loving your neighbor as you do yourself. When I've gotten into a heated place with my husband, my flesh told me, "Don't cook him another meal, and don't wash so much as a sock for him." However, my not cooking means he could go out to eat and blow our budget to smithereens. Not washing his clothes means that I will be stuck with laundry piled up until I decide to get to it. So for me, it's not worth it.

As you go throughout your day, ask yourself how the choices you make are going to impact your life and the life of someone else. If the answer comes back negative, don't do it. Let the love of God flow in your life, and it will automatically flow to others. God bless you!

Today's Scripture: Mark 12:30–31.

Today's Prayer/Confession: I love myself too much to allow myself to step outside of the love of God. God's law of love is the highest law there is, and I submit myself to it completely!

Build Your Platform

Inheriting the promises of God is no easy feat, but there is a way to receive all God has promised us. I was reading Hebrews 11, which I consider the Hall of Faith, filling myself with all that those who have gone before us have accomplished. Each had the same testimony. They pleased God with their faith, and as a result, inherited His promise.

I remember a story about David Paul Yonggi Cho, pastor of one of the world's largest churches in Seoul, Korea. In the early days of his ministry, he didn't have transportation. At that time, a bicycle was an absolute luxury and few people could afford one. Pastor Cho decided he was going to pray and believe in God for a bike. He prayed the prayer of faith and received the bike in his heart. He had a mental picture of the bike in a particular corner of his house, so every day he rejoiced and praised God for answering his prayer.

He went to church and shared that God had given him a bike, and because they were not easy to come by, his friends were eager to see the bike. Pastor Cho agreed to allow them into his home to view his bike. When they arrived, he took them to the empty corner and his friends mocked him, saying, "We knew you were lying. There is no bike here."

Cho replied, "Yes, there is!"

But his friends insisted, "No, there isn't. We don't see a bike, so you don't have one."

Pastor Cho's response was, "My friends, I received my bike by faith in my heart the day I prayed, and unfortunately, until you can first see it in your inner man, you will never see it out here." His friends left in disbelief that Cho would make up such a story, not sure how it came to be but shortly after, they were amazed when Pastor Cho came riding his new bike onto the church grounds.

When you make the choice to believe God for something, you have to be able to see yourself with it before you have it. In Mark 11, Jesus said, *"Believe you receive when you pray and you will have it."* The believing part should be taken care of before you ever ask. There has to be an inward conviction that what you desire is already yours. This is why so many people struggle to receive from God. They allow their desire to drive their mouths to jump ahead of their hearts, and they ask but don't receive.

Your heart must be full of faith before you ask. You have to have a firm, confident conviction (belief) that God will do what He has promised. Never ask before you believe. Never!

Asking is like building a platform. When there is something that you desire, it may take days, weeks, or even months to fill your heart and mind with the Word of God in that area. Quote scripture throughout the day, listen to the Bible on CD while you sleep or in the car, talk scripture over with family and friends, and so on. What are you doing? You're getting the Word deep in your heart, ensuring that you believe and have enough support to stand on. You are building a platform in preparation to ask. Eventually the scriptures will begin speaking to you (Proverbs 6:22). That's when you have the assurance that you already have it and your heart has become full of faith. Now you're ready to ask. When you go into prayer, you step up on the platform of the Word of God because you believe it. It is deep in your heart, so you open your mouth and ask.

Whenever I have asked under these conditions, I have always received the petitions that I desire of Him (1 John 3:22). It has never failed. It may have taken some time, but God always came through. Yes, it's a time consuming process, and many don't want to work through it, but it's so worth it when you receive the answer to your prayers!

I once heard someone say there are 11,000 promises in the Bible. I don't know if that is true, but I do know there are many that have yet to be appropriated. Are you ready? Let's find ourselves like the men and women of old who walked by faith and not by sight! Let's inherit all of the promises of God!

God bless you. Have an anointed day!

Today's Scriptures: Hebrews 11; Proverbs 6:22; 1 John 3:22.

Today's Prayer/Confession: Father, I thank you that I can inherit your promises by using your Word. Abraham believed you and you credited it to him as righteousness. I believe you, and I know that you will hold true to your Word for me just as you did Abraham. You are no respecter of persons. Thank you for giving us your Word to stand on. It's our firm foundation. In Jesus's name, Amen!

Understanding Matthew 6:33

For the last thirty years, I have heard Matthew 6:33 preached in a way that left the impression that if I simply "seek the Kingdom of God (spiritual things) and His righteousness, all things (natural things, i.e., cars, houses, land, money) will be added unto me." That was so entrenched in my mind that I rarely, if ever, asked for natural things. God already knew what I desired, so my part was busying myself advancing His Kingdom and His part was to just add what I wanted. Sounded like a winning combination to me.

I started to take inventory of my life and began to notice that although God has been good to me, most of the natural things I desired, I added to myself. I thought about my house, my car, and my other possessions, and realized I had worked hard on my job and kept my credit scores high so when I wanted things, I could get them for myself. None of them were just added to me. Again, yes, it was God's goodness. I don't diminish that at all, but I went after those things on my own.

When you think about adding to someone, it's giving without any effort or toil on the part of the recipient. For example, I was in the store the other day shopping for an item I needed for my home when I saw a beautiful little dress for my daughter. She wasn't with me, but I wanted her to have the dress, so I bought it and gave it to her. What did I do? I added it to her. She didn't ask for it and she didn't work for it. Nothing was required from her. All she needed to do was receive it, and she did. She thanked me and went on her merry little way.

In Matthew 6:25–33 it says this:

Therefore I say unto you, Take no thought for your life, what ye shall eat, or what ye shall drink; nor yet for your body, what ye shall put on ... Therefore take no thought, saying, What shall we eat? or, What shall we drink? Or, Wherewithal shall we be clothed? (For after all these things do the Gentiles seek) for your heavenly Father knoweth that ye have need of all these things. But seek ye first the kingdom of God, and his righteousness; and all these things shall be added unto you.

Jesus clearly stated that there were three things that will be "added" to us when we seek the Kingdom—food, clothing, and drink. He didn't mention anything else. So where did the idea come from that He would just add anything else? I don't know, and I can't tell you how this messed up my theology because I wanted God to add every *thing* to me, just as I did my daughter's dress. I didn't have a problem using my faith for spiritual things, but natural things weren't on my list. I didn't want to think about where I would live and what I would drive. I wanted God to busy Himself with that. He knows my taste and He's a good Father, so I wanted Him to just bless me with the things I desired. I didn't want to think about them, so I found myself waiting for God only to discover that all this time God was waiting for me.

God is true to His Word, and neither I nor my children have ever worried about a meal, drink, or our clothing. We haven't always been able to eat, drink, or wear whatever we wanted, but every day of our lives God has provided in those three areas, and He did so without any effort on our part, just as He said He would in Matthew 6.

So what happens with the things we desire that are not food, drink, or clothes? How do we get those things? We have to possess them by using our faith, plain and simple. God promised to give us the desires of our heart after we have delighted ourselves in Him, and that takes faith (Psalms 37:4). He promised that we would be perfect and entire, wanting nothing, after our position of faith had been tried (James 1:4). He promised that we would receive, but only after we released our faith by believing and praying (Mark 11). Yes, God is the one granting the desires, but to receive from Him outside of Matthew 6:33, you will have to activate your faith. It's a prerequisite. I'm not implying that faith isn't needed for Matthew 6:33, because it is. Everything we do takes faith. When we use our faith, we lay hold of all that God has promised.

I pray this helps you today! Remember God is waiting for you!

Today's Scriptures: Matthew 6:25–33; Psalms 37:4; James 1:4; Mark 11:22–24.

Today's Prayer/Confession: Father, help me walk in a place where I can receive all you have provided for me. I won't worry myself with food, drink, or clothing, because you promised to add those things if I sought your kingdom. I commit to using the faith you have given me to appropriate all of your promises, so my life can be a channel of blessing to others. In Jesus's name I pray, Amen!

All Grace

This is a season of growing in absolute trust in God and His word. There are many things I have before the Lord concerning my family, ministry, and much more. If allowed, these areas can become so overwhelming they yell for my attention. If I look in their direction, it can bring discouragement, and if I keep looking for too long, it will cause me to waver in unbelief (Romans 4:20). When I fail to take my eyes off the circumstances and place them on the Word of God, my faith is greatly hindered.

Recently I was in a situation where everything around me seemed to be caving in—my children, family, ministry, everything. I was thinking, "Lord, how do I continue doing all that I'm doing? Where am I missing it? How do I keep everything together while at the same time fulfilling the call that you have placed on my life? How do I do this, Lord?" What was happening to me? I had my eyes on the circumstances.

I was battling thoughts of discouragement faster than I could blink when suddenly these words came to me: *"And God is able to make all grace abound toward you; that ye, always having all sufficiency in all things, may abound to every good work."* It was 2 Corinthians 9:8. I knew it was in the Bible, but I hadn't thought about it as it relates to my life. I felt the urge to say it out loud: "God is able to make *all* grace abound toward me, *all grace abound to me, all grace abound to me, all grace abound to me!*" I said those words until a light came on in my inner man. The words weren't coming from my head; they were coming from my spirit. So I kept saying and thinking about them, turning them over and over in my mind.

Do you know that *all* means "all," and it leaves nothing out? The word *grace* means "favor, benefit, and reward". Put those words together and it says that God is able to make every favor and reward *that He possesses* come to me. Not just some of it, but all of it! Everybody loves it when someone does them a favor, but God's favor exceeds them all. He is willing to extend all of His benefits to you! Imagine that!

The Amplified translation of 2 Corinthians 9:8 says it like this:

*And **God is able** to **make all grace** (every favor and earthly blessing) come to you in abundance, so that you may always and under **all** circumstances and whatever the need be self-sufficient [possessing enough to require no aid* *or support and furnished in abundance for every good work and charitable donation].*

To quote something I overheard a four-year-old boy in our church say, "That's tight!"

Have a great day!

Today's Scriptures: Romans 4:20; 2 Corinthians 9:8.

Today's Prayer/Confession: And God is able to make all grace (every favor and earthly blessing) come to me in abundance, so that I may always, and under all circumstances and whatever the need, be self-sufficient, possessing enough to require no aid or support and furnished in abundance for every good work and charitable donation. In Jesus's name, Amen!

You Are an Overcomer

Satan is a name all of us are acquainted with. John called him "the accuser of the brethren" and "angel of the bottomless pit" (Revelation 12:10 and 9:11). Jesus called him "the wicked one," "the unclean spirit," and "the father of lies" (Matthew 12:43, Matthew 13:19, and John 8:44). Isaiah called him a "crooked Serpent" and "dragon" (Isaiah 27:1). Paul called him the "god of this world" and "the tempter" (1 Thessalonians 3:5 and 2 Corinthians 4:4).

It honestly doesn't matter whether he's called Satan, the devil, or the enemy; we all know who he is, and if you have been a Christian for any period of time, you have experienced him in action. Although he comes with a lot of names and titles, Jesus defeated him, and unless you give him place, he is absolutely powerless in your life. So the title he carries above them all is *Defeated and Overcome.*

As a Christian, you can't focus your attention on the works of the devil. I don't care how bad he can make things look. If you keep your eyes fixed on the Word of God, you are guaranteed the victory. We are told in 1 John 3:8 that Jesus was brought forth so that he could undo the works of the devil. The works of the devil, according to John 10:10 include killing, stealing, and destroying. Jesus came to undo these works for you. "Undoing" is like untying a person bound with ropes. Jesus came and removed all the ropes Satan had in our lives, and he didn't just undo them, he destroyed them so they were no longer a threat to us. Unfortunately, many of us put those ropes back on, and we do it with the words of our mouth.

Because we are accustomed to living in the natural realm, we have been trained to say what we see. We "tell it like it is." The problem with that is Jesus specifically told us in Mark 11 that we would have whatsoever we say. He also said in Matthew 12:36 that we would have to give an account for every idle word we speak. God's desire is that the words of our mouth produce favorable results in our lives. An idle word is an unproductive, empty word. In order to walk in the reality of an overcoming life, your words will have to agree with God. According to 1 John 2:14, we have overcome the wicked one. Is he overcome in your life?

Overcoming started with Jesus. He paid the price and positioned you to be an overcomer. An overcomer is one who conquers, one who prevails. It's our responsibility to stand tall in the position we have been given. Revelation 12:11 states that we overcome the enemy with two things: the blood of the lamb and the word of our testimony. Jesus took care of the first part and now it's up to you and me to lock in on the second—the word of our testimony.

I don't know why God has designed the words of our mouth to bring us into victory, but He did. I would rather obey Him and get results than to reason and live a defeated life. To say what God has said is the key to victory. If we say what we see, we will continue to have what we see. But through the power of the Holy Spirit, if we speak what we desire, the words of our mouth will change the course of things. So say it loud and say it strong. Jesus and all of heaven is backing us up. I am an overcomer!

God bless you today!

Today's Scriptures: Revelation 9:11, 12:10–11; Matthew 12:36, 43, 13:19; John 8:44; Isaiah 27:1; 1 Thessalonians 3:5; 2 Corinthians 4:4; 1 John 2:14, 3:8; John 10:10.

Today's Prayer/Confession: Father, let the words of my mouth agree with your Word. I speak as an overcomer and will not allow the works of the devil to be my focus. I put pressure on my tongue to say what your Word says, and I know that I will have the victory in Jesus's name, Amen!

If It's Forfeited, It's Mine!

"A good man leaves an inheritance to his children's children: and the wealth of the sinner is laid up for the just" (Proverbs 13:22). I used to hear this passage of scripture and think, "That's not fair." Why would God allow any persons, saved or sinner, to work all their lives by the sweat of their brow only to end up turning their wealth over to someone else? Yes, there are benefits to being a believer, but something in my mind couldn't wrap around the idea of the righteous gaining what others had labored for. So I studied this passage of scripture and found that the word *sinner* in Proverbs 13:22 comes from the Hebrew word *"chata,"* which means "to miss the mark." It also means "to wander away from or to forfeit." That shed light on the subject for me.

I had previously thought this passage meant that God was taking from the sinner and giving it to the righteous. After a careful study, I realized that sinners forfeit what rightfully belongs to them. God doesn't take it. They wander away from it. When someone forfeits something, they abandon it through negligence or breach of contract. The dictionary defines *forfeit* as "a violation; to lose the right to and open up one's possession to seizure." Now I understand.

When people choose to neglect or abandon the wealth or substance given to them by God, it leaves it open to someone else possessing or seizing it. That is what happens when the wealth of the sinner ends up in the hands of the just. We are not forcing our way in and taking it, it's being left for our possession. It is like a man traveling on a road not searching for anything, yet finding priceless treasures along the way. Others have walked the same road but found nothing because the treasures were hidden. That's what it means when something is "laid up." It is hidden *for* us, not *from* us. It is hidden from those who have not accepted the finished work of justification and hidden for those who have.

So how do we benefit? By feeding on God's Word and allowing the Word to direct our steps. Psalms 119:105 says: *"Thy word is a lamp unto my feet and a light unto my path."* The Word of God will show you where to walk. If you obey and take the path set before you, you will never have to search for the substance of the sinner. It will glisten, shimmer, and shine as you travel your God-given path.

Have a great day!

Today's Scriptures: Proverbs 13:22; Psalms 119:105.

Today's Prayer/Confession: Father, your Word says that the steps of the good man are ordered by the Lord. I believe this is true, and I ask that you make me sensitive to the steps you have ordered for my life. I place my focus on you and your Word. I will not seek after the wealth of the sinner, but I thank you that it automatically finds its way into my hands. I am a possessor of all that you have promised. In Jesus's name! Amen!

The Contrary Winds Won't Stop You

In the earth's atmosphere there are many types of winds, and all fit into one of two categories: global or local. These winds, totaling about 138 are felt all over the world's atmosphere. Some are calm summer breezes, while others have been known to destroy entire countries. However, no wind can be as devastating as what the Bible calls a contrary wind.

And when even was come, the ship was in the midst of the sea, and he alone on the land. And he saw them toiling in rowing; for the wind was contrary unto them: and about the fourth watch of the night he cometh unto them, walking upon the sea, and would have passed by them. But when they saw him walking upon the sea, they supposed it had been a spirit, and cried out: For they all saw him, and were troubled. And immediately he talked with them, and saith unto them, Be of good cheer: it is I; be not afraid. And he went up unto them into the ship; and the wind ceased. (Mark 6:47–51)

A contrary wind is a force that positions itself against us; it is a hostile, adversary wind with a mission to stop us from accomplishing what God has instructed us to do. It originates with the enemy, and its target is the mind or the heart. It blows words or thoughts of negativity, opposition, and discouragement, but we can never forget that no matter how hard the wind may blow, Jesus is always with us, and just as he did with the disciples at sea, he will quiet and still the storms in our lives.

If we learn to put our absolute trust in Jesus, no matter how the winds may blow, we can stand confident that no weapon fashioned against us will be able to stand. Jesus saw the disciples "toiling in rowing," which means he saw them working hard to avoid drowning, and he came to their rescue. He wasn't going to let them go under. He took care of the situation.

The goal of a contrary wind is to feed you negative or bad reports in order to shake you and get you off your position of faith. It wants you to move away from trusting God. But in 2 Thessalonians 2:2, Paul said this: *"Now, we beseech you, brethren, by the coming of our Lord Jesus Christ ... That ye be not soon shaken in mind, or be troubled, neither by spirit, nor by word, nor by letter as from us, as that the day of Christ is at hand."* The Message Bible says: *"Don't let anyone shake you up or get you excited over some breathless report."*

Because we live in a sinful world, negative things are going to happen, you are going to hear and see things that will impact your life in a negative way. But our response should never be like the world's response. Our hope is in Christ. He is our rock and our salvation (Psalms 18:2), and He is the help we look to in times of trouble. The winds may blow but they won't knock our lives down because our lives are founded on *The Rock* (Matthew 7:25). Have a great day!

Today's Scriptures: Mark 6:47–51; 2 Thessalonians 2:2; Psalms 18:2; Matthew 7:25.

Today's Prayer/Confession: I will not allow the circumstances of life to blow me away. My life is founded on The Rock, which is Christ. I will not fall! I will not fail! God is with me, and He won't allow contrary winds to overcome my life!

Discipline Is Not a Nasty Word

Some people struggle with being overweight and others struggle with being underweight. For a period of time in my life, I struggled with being underweight. I remember often asking myself, "Did you eat today?" The answer was usually, "No." I had become so busy that I failed to discipline myself to sit down and have a decent meal.

During that time, I weighed less than one hundred pounds and could barely keep on a size zero. I made the choice to seek the Lord for help. I was led to eat a piece of toast every day and drink water throughout the day. Believe it or not, it took great discipline for me. It was a battle because my mind would tell me that I didn't want to eat, and my body would seem to agree. I would feel nauseous at the thought of eating, but I forced myself to eat and would say to my body, "You are going to take this toast and you are not going to reject it. It is going to stay in your stomach." There were days that I would hate to think about the next time I had to eat because of the way it made me feel. But I kept at it in spite of how I felt. I would not listen to the voice of my body, and it paid off for me in the end. It was hard, but I did what I needed to do, because I wanted to have a long, healthy life.

Discipline might sound like a nasty word, but it's not. The Bible interchanges the word discipline with chastening or correction. It is the tool God uses to bring us to a place of greatness. If anyone understands discipline, it is the United States Marine Corps. This is their definition: "Discipline is the instant willingness and obedience to all orders, respect for authority, self-reliance, and teamwork. The ability to do the right thing, even when no one is watching, or suffer the consequences of guilt, which produces pain in our bodies. Through pain comes discipline."

No one wants to suffer, but if we don't set boundaries in our lives, regardless of the price we have to pay, we will regret it. If you look at your life and there are areas that seem "out of control," it is probably due to a lack of discipline. God wants discipline in every area, spiritual as well as natural, because the exercise of discipline builds our character. It shapes us into all God wants us to be. It is essential if we desire to fulfill God's call on our lives, and without it, we will never reach the levels of greatness we are destined for.

Who wants a surgeon who didn't discipline himself to learn his profession? Who wants a pastor who didn't discipline himself to study the Word of God? Who wants a lawyer representing him who didn't take the time to educate himself on their case? No one does. Everyone wants a professional. When you take the time to discipline yourself, you position yourself to be a professional at life.

In Revelation 3:19, Jesus said that those He loves, He disciplines and corrects. Don't despise His discipline. Make yourself do what you know you need to do. Don't allow yourself to be held back with thoughts like "It's too hard," or "It hurts too much." Pay the price now so you can enjoy life later.

Have a powerful day!

Today's Scriptures: Proverbs 19:18; Hebrews 12:6; Revelation 3:19.

Today's Prayer/Confession: Father, help me to discipline myself so I can be all you desire me to be. Help me to say "No" in times of weakness so I can walk in the blessings that you have in store for my life. In Jesus's name, Amen!

His Voice is The Voice

In this day and time, it is important that we learn to shut out the voices around us and listen. I was in a season of "cocooning" myself with the Word of God, constantly listening to messages by others via CD, the Internet, or heart-to-hearts with friends. My ears and heart were open to hear what God had to say. I refused to leave an opening for negativity, the persuasions of the enemy, or my own carnality. I was bombarding my mind and heart with others to drown out the enemy.

One day, the Lord spoke to me and said, "My voice is The Voice that you want to hear. Make sure that you leave an opening for my voice."

"Yes, Sir", I replied.

Now is the time to listen to The Voice—the Voice of God. In 1 Corinthians 14:10, we are told: "*There are, it may be, so many kinds of voices in the world, and none of them is without signification.*" *Signification* in this sense means "importance, purpose, or consequence." In other words, all of the voices in the world have something to say. They all have a purpose, and they all have a destination they are trying to reach inside our hearts, so it is imperative that we (on purpose) drown them out and tune our spiritual ears to The Voice of God. We must have ears to hear what the Spirit of God has to say to us. His voice is the necessary voice of the hour.

One day I checked my phone history, which tells me who I spoke with and how long. I was amazed that I could spend so many hours on the phone listening to others, yet struggle in my flesh to settle down long enough to hear The Voice of the Father. His voice comes to us continuously, but other voices can be so loud that they drown out The Voice of God. This is why it's very easy to hear the Lord speaking to us early in the morning, or sometimes during the late hours of the evening. Most of the activity in the world has stopped, and the silence in the atmosphere gives way to The Voice of the Lord. We have to train ourselves to become more sensitive to His voice all day, every day, and not just during the early or late watches of the night. God is speaking, but are you listening?

Training yourself to hear is not hard. In Philippians 4:12, Paul said, "*I know both how to be abased and how to abound.*" Although he was talking about his financial condition, I think it applies here also. Being abased is knowing when and how to bring yourself low. It's an act of humility.

Silencing your voice and those of others, in my opinion, is being abased, because you are positioning yourself "under" in order to hear from the Master who is positioned over you.

When we learn to quiet ourselves and come into His presence, we will change in ways we never expected. His voice gives direction for the course of our lives and fills us with the wisdom and knowledge necessary to accomplish our God-given task. Let's abound in hearing His voice and become the recipients of God's greater blessings.

Have a blessed day!

Today's Scriptures: 1 Corinthians 14:10; Philippians 4:12.

Today's Prayer/Confession: Today I will quiet myself and the voices of others in order to hear The Voice of God. I am sensitive to Him, and I can clearly hear every word that He speaks to me!

My Heart to His Eyes

Not too long ago, my husband and I were doing an altar call, which is a time of personal prayer, surrender, and humility. As I walked the platform, I noticed a few individuals who were at the altar solely because they were told to come. Their posture made it clear that their time at the altar was wasted, and the words spoken had no place in their heart. So I began talking to them about the dangers of a callous heart.

A callous heart is hard and insensitive to the things of God. It's not impressed with godly things. God can be moving in a powerful way, but the heart can't receive because it's imprisoned by its own stony walls. In the Old Testament, God was continuously dealing with Israel about this very thing. He didn't just say their hearts were hard, but He said their necks were stiff, which meant they were stubborn and difficult to deal with. Don't let this be the case with you.

If there is any area of your life that God has endeavored to deal with and you are turning that area of your life away from Him, eventually your heart will become callous. Any area that is callous is an area that God can't access and change. You can love Him and still make places of your heart off limits to Him. Because He's a perfect gentleman, He will not violate your will or bypass what you have marked as "off limits." God will stay out of that area of your life. But don't ever forget that any place in your heart held back from Him will become a place that will eventually cause great trouble in your life. The Word of God says that a heart that is hard and unrepentant stores up terrible punishment for itself (Roman 2:5).

One of the quickest ways to discover if your heart is callous is to check your attitude. Are you open to allowing someone to talk with you about a specific area of your life, or do you find a reason to quickly leave and end the discussion? Is walking away from that area an option for you if God requires it? If the answer is no, there is a heart condition.

I remember being in a relationship with a young man I was certain would be my husband. The very thought of not having him in my life was more than I was willing to embrace, so whenever the thought came, I would ignore it and find a way to spend more time with him. The longer I ignored it, the deeper my emotional ties became and the harder my heart grew toward God. Eventually everything that could possibly go wrong went wrong, and I suffered greatly because I failed to keep my heart open to God. To this day, I carry scars from that relationship, but thank God I'm free of it!

Your heart must be protected at all costs. Proverbs 4:23 says: *"Keep thy heart with all diligence, for out of it are the issues of life."* If the forces of life flow from our hearts, we can't afford to allow anything to build around it, stopping the flow of God's Spirit in our lives. One translation says, "Above all that you prize, make sure to keep a watch over your heart, for out of it springs the forces of life."

In Psalms 18:24, King David said this: *"God rewrote the text of my life when I opened the book of my heart to his eyes"* (Message). Keep your heart pliable and sensitive to God, being quick to repent and making the proper adjustments. Allow the eyes of God to always have access to the book of your heart.

Have a great day!

Today's Scriptures: Romans 2:5; Proverbs 4:23; Psalms 18:24.

Today's Prayer/Confession: Father, I want my heart to be open to you. I will not block any area of my life. You have access to it all. Make me who you have called me to be, and keep my heart pliable and sensitive to you. In Jesus's name, Amen!

You Are an Ambassador

One day I was listening as a minister shared his experiences on the mission field. The country he had visited was one of the poorest countries in the world, and as he ventured out he was overwhelmed by the living conditions of the village people. They were eating garbage as flies swarmed around them. He continued his journey, taking in the horrific conditions of the country, when he suddenly came upon a beautiful gated home with a superbly manicured lawn and flowers all around the grounds. He was shocked. The contrast was so great that he asked in amazement, "What is that and who lives there?!"

The driver said, "That is the home of the U.S. ambassador."

The minister was almost angry, thinking about the way the people were living in contrast to the way the U.S ambassador lived. Then the Holy Spirit spoke to him and said, "This is what it means to be in the world, but not of the world" (John 17:15–19).

Jesus had made this statement prior to His crucifixion. He was praying with the foreknowledge that everyone who chose to follow Him would have to live in a world ravaged by sin, full of the works of the devil—killing, stealing, and destroying (John 10:10). He also knew that through Him, those of us in the world would have the power and ability to live a life of abundance right in the midst of the conditions of the world. We don't conform to the world. We win and it is not predicated on what is going on in the world around us.

We are in the world, but not of the world. The word *of* means "from," and the word *world* is the Greek word *"Kosmos,"* which is a governing system ruled by Satan designed to bind and control those living in it. Jesus said we are not from the *Kosmos* or world system. In Colossians 1:13 (NLT), Paul tells us where we *are* from: *"For he has rescued us from the kingdom of darkness and transferred us into the Kingdom of his dear Son."*

We are from a higher Kingdom. The Kingdom of God and the power of that Kingdom override the kingdom and rulers of the world. It doesn't matter what the conditions are around us, the power of our King and Kingdom will change how it affects us. If that U.S. ambassador has a need, he is not going to look to the people in the country in which he's stationed. His need is met by the country he came from.

It's the same for you and me. When we have needs in our lives, we call out to our Father, who is our resource. The Bible says in Philippians 4:19: *"God shall supply all your need according to His riches in glory, by Christ Jesus."* He's not going to meet our need by the area or system we live in, but by the riches of the Kingdom He dwells in. That means that our needs will be met on a higher level than what the world has to offer. What the world offers will bind us, but what God offers frees us!

"The blessing of the Lord, it maketh rich, and he addeth no sorrow with it" (Proverbs 10:22).

Live your life out of the Kingdom that you have come from. 2 Corinthians 5:20 says we are Ambassadors for Christ, so don't be governed by the system around you. Feed on the Word of God so that you can see what is rightfully yours. The days of a poverty mentality are over. God wants the blessing of His Kingdom in operation in every area of your life, but you have to get the truth of the Word of God about your Kingdom to walk in it. Don't let the system of the world hold you down. Break out and let the world see that although the enemy may have come to steal, kill, and destroy, Jesus came that we might have and enjoy life, in abundance to the full, until it overflows. When they see this, they will quickly leave the system of the world and flood the Kingdom of God's dear Son!

This is the beginning of a new day for you! Have a powerful day!

Today's Scriptures: John 17:15–19; John 10:10; Colossians 1:13; Philippians 4:19; Proverbs 10:22; 2 Corinthians 5:20.

Today's Prayer/Confession: I have been translated out of the kingdom of darkness into the Kingdom of God's dear Son. I am an Ambassador of the Kingdom of God, living in a land that is not my home. My life is filled with the power of the Kingdom of God, and my light shines brightly to bless others!

Stand Your Ground and Fight

Yesterday my husband jogged my memory as he was sharing the comical yet very true story of our youngest son, Kyle. Kyle was about five years old when our neighbors moved in. They had a son named Moses, who was two years older than Kyle. Moses picked on Kyle every chance he got, so eventually if Kyle was outside playing and Moses showed up, we would hear Kyle running into the house. Moses would hit him and push him or force Kyle into being his "little flunky." The way he spoke to Kyle gave the impression that he thought Kyle was beneath him. I wanted Kyle to handle it and saw an excellent opportunity to teach my son about the dynamics of walking in love. You know, turn the other cheek (Matthew 5:39), enduring long, take no account of the evil being done (1 Corinthians 13:4–8 Amplified). In all honesty, I just didn't want my baby fighting.

I thought my husband was with me. He never said a word when I talked with Kyle, and I thought he was in agreement with what I was saying. But I discovered the truth. My husband went along with my instructions because he wanted peace, but he was eventually forced to give Kyle a different set of instructions. My husband told Kyle in private, "Son, don't you allow anyone to treat you like this. Now I know what your mother has told you, and what she said is true. We don't want you picking fights, but I'm telling you to do what you need to do to get Moses off of you." The words of his father empowered Kyle. He listened, and the next time we saw Moses and Kyle together, Kyle was chasing Moses with a tree branch yelling, "My daddy said I don't have to take this from you anymore!" I can assure you that Kyle hasn't had any further problems with Moses.

Sometimes you have got to let the enemy know, "My Heavenly Father said I don't have to take this from you anymore!" I learned a great lesson from both my husband and my son. Love is not wimpy, and real love won't allow you to be taken advantage of. My husband loved my son enough to give him a balanced message. You don't run from your enemy, especially one that means you harm. To settle the issue, you are going to have to stand and fight.

"Finally, my brethren, be strong in the Lord, and in the power of his might. Put on the whole armour of God, that ye may be able to stand against the wiles of the devil" (Ephesians 6:10–11).

The word *wiles* means "strategies or tactics." We have God's armour to stand against the strategies and tactics of the devil. If we choose not to put it on, the enemy will walk all over us, and this has been going on far too long. There are too many Christians running from the enemy, hiding afraid and tormented. The devil has no authority in your life. Jesus took his authority (Matthew 28:18) and he can only influence your life to the degree that you allow. He comes to us with thoughts, ideas, and suggestions, and he wants you to believe that he's more powerful than God and has more authority than we do. But he is not and he does not.

Mark 12:36 says the enemies of Jesus are to be made His footstool. You put your foot on a footstool, and that's the true image you need to have of the enemy. His voice and influence belong under your feet. Don't run from the devil. Receive the word of the Father, and walk in the reality of His Word. When you do, you will never have another day of defeat. You were created to win and reign, not run (Romans 5:17). Determine today that he can no longer have his way in your life, because you have, like Kyle, a Word from your heavenly Father!

Have a great day!

Today's Scriptures: Matthew 5:39; 1 Corinthians 13:4–8; Ephesians 6:10–11; Matthew 28:18; Mark 12:36; Romans 5:17.

Today's Prayer/Confession: Today is a day of victory for me. I will not run in the face of opposition. I will stand my ground and fight the good fight of faith. God has promised me victory through my Lord and Savior Jesus Christ!

Keep on Pushing

There was a time in my life when I wouldn't finish anything. If I started washing dishes, when I got to the pots and pans, I would walk away and do something else. If I made my bed, I would pull the covers over half the bed, keep lumps in the middle, and leave out straightening the pillows. I wasn't a finisher. As I got older and became more focused in my walk with Christ, I didn't realize that the practice of not finishing carried over into my spiritual life, and as my husband often says, "If we are not watchful, practice on any level will make permanent." I was perfecting the art of not finishing.

About seven years ago, my husband and I were throwing around the idea of buying a new home. We found one in a beautiful area with plenty of land. The moment we stepped onto the grounds of this house, we were both excited and made the decision that we would use our faith and believe God to help us secure the house. We held hands and used Matthew 18:19: *"If two of you shall agree on earth as touching anything that they shall ask, it shall be done for them of my Father which is in heaven."* We both said "Amen," and as far as we were concerned, it was a done deal. Every day we quoted Matthew 18:19, Mark 11:22–25, and other scriptures just to keep ourselves in a place of faith.

Somewhere along the way, I began to mentally process what the house would cost us. Although we could afford it, I just didn't want a really high mortgage payment, so thoughts of the mortgage payment began to loosen my spiritual grip on the house. I never said a word to my husband, but internally I had released the house. I didn't finish the course. I just let it go.

Weeks went by, and one day my husband turned to me and said, "Melva, did you let go of the house?" He could sense the disconnection. I stood there with this *Well, see what had happened was …* look on my face. As long as I live, I will never forget the disappointment in my husband's eyes. He later said to me, "If you had just shared where you were, I could have walked with you and strengthened my own faith, but you just left me out there holding this thing by myself and you never said a word. Don't ever do that again. When we stand before God to believe for something, we both have to walk it through all the way to the end. So count up the cost before you put your agreement to it or you will never possess the things that God has for your life." Whew! Need I say more? That day I became an official finisher.

When we become Christians, our entire walk is to be lived out by faith. Hebrews 12:2 calls Jesus the Author and Finisher of our faith. Another way to say it would be that Jesus is the initiator and the completer of our faith. He takes it all the way to the end. What if Jesus had started out going to the cross and just before He died, He changed His mind and said, "You know what, Father, I'm coming down. I changed my mind. These people just don't get it." You and I would have been doomed, and the plan of Salvation would never have come into being. But thank God He didn't change His mind. He is the Author and the Finisher. He doesn't stop midstream and go in another direction. Jesus is our example. If He was a finisher, we have to be finishers.

If you started out believing God for something and you stopped midstream, get back in faith. Be persistent like the woman sick with an issue of blood in Mark 5:25. She was willing to go the extra mile to get to Jesus; through bad doctors, bankruptcy, religious systems, and crowds of people she pressed to get what she needed from the Lord. She didn't allow her condition or the circumstances around her to cause her to abort her mission to receive her healing. Don't let circumstances cause you to abort your mission, either.

God's plan in you is a great plan, and it will come to pass if you make up your mind to finish the course. Then you will one day be able to say, like the Apostle Paul in 2 Timothy 4:7, "*I have fought a good fight, I have FINISHED my course, I have kept the faith.*"

I'll close today's Manna using a few words from the song "Keep on Pushing" by singer/songwriter, Curtis Mayfield. It will serve as today's confession.

I've got to keep on pushing
I can't stop now
Move up a little higher
Some way, somehow
Cause I've got my strength
And it don't make sense
Not to keep on pushin'

Keep on pushin' and have an awesome day!

Today's Scriptures: Matthew 18:19; Mark 11:22–25; Hebrews 12:2; 2 Timothy 4:7.

Let the Word Rise in Your Life Today!

I woke this morning hearing these words: "The Word must increase in your home." My husband and I have always been "Word people," and it's not often that you won't find us feeding on something to build or strengthen our spirits, yet the Holy Spirit was saying, "Around your family and in your home the Word of God needs to increase." Does this apply also to you? What is the spiritual climate around you and in your home? If you study the scriptures, you find certain places where there was a shortage of the Word of God and wherever there was a shortage, there was also an absence of victory, healing, and provision. Simply put, there were very few manifestations of God.

In 2 Chronicles 17, a man named Jehoshaphat became the king of Judah. He recognized that something was wrong, because the people were doing things and living in ways that did not line up with the laws of God. To change the situation, the Message Bible says, *"Jehoshaphat got rid of the people's local sex-and-religious shrines."* These were God's chosen people, those delivered from Egypt, not Gentile nations. But something was missing, and Jehoshaphat clearly saw what it was.

> *In the third year of his reign he sent his officials—excellent men, every one of them ... on a teaching mission to the cities of Judah. They were accompanied by Levites ... and the priests ... were also in the company. They made a circuit of the towns of Judah, teaching the people and using the Book of The Revelation of God as their text.* (2 Chronicles 17:7–9, The Message)

Jehoshaphat recognized that there was a lack of knowledge in God's ways and laws among the people. Their lifestyles proved it. The older generation had forgotten and the younger generation hadn't learned, so they were engaging in activities forbidden in the Word of God. Jehoshaphat's answer was to send men out from town to town with one purpose—to bring an awareness of the laws of God to the people. What was he doing? Jehoshaphat was increasing the ministry of the Word of God.

Not long after, verses 10–13 say:

There was a strong sense of the fear of God in all the kingdoms around

Judah—they didn't dare go to war against Jehoshaphat. Some Philistines even brought gifts and a load of silver to Jehoshaphat, and the desert Bedouin brought flocks—7,700 rams and 7,700 goats. So Jehoshaphat became stronger by the day, and constructed more and more forts and store-cities—an age of prosperity for Judah! (2 Chronicles 17:10–13, The Message)

What happened? The Word of God was increased and the lives of the people changed! The text says they became stronger by the day. Their lives changed so much and so fast that it brought fear to the nations around them. They watched as Judah grew in strength and numbers. They saw the abundance flowing in their towns "by the day" as they had never seen before, and it caused great fear to come on them, and no one dared to fight against them. Whenever the Word is taught on a consistent level, it raises the hearers to a higher place in life. Jehoshaphat didn't have to kill anyone to get the spoils of his enemy. They came and dropped it at his feet all because of the increase of God's Word.

God wants us to be enveloped by His Word, so no matter in what direction you look or turn, you are surrounded by the Word of God! His Word is to rise in your life, but you are the only one who can cause it to do so. Don't go another day without the power of the Word in your atmosphere. The Word is God's wisdom. It's the source God uses to bring you to a place of peace, increase, overflow, and abundance. Proverbs 8:21 states that wisdom causes those that love it to inherit substance, and it fills their lives with treasures. God's Word is God's wisdom. Let it rise in your life today!

Today's Scriptures: 2 Chronicles 17:7–13; Proverbs 8:21.

Today's Prayer/Confession: Today I will increase the Word in my atmosphere. I will give the Word of God first place in my life and allow it to bring me to a place of peace and prosperity with nothing missing and nothing broken. In Jesus's name, Amen!

Just Believe God!

You need healing in your body so you asked God for it. You used the Word, prayed, and received in your heart, but as you wait for the manifestation, the doctor's report gets worse. What do you do?

You asked God to save a loved one. You rejoice over His promises, knowing that salvation is for your entire household. You received the answer in your heart, but as you waited for the manifestation, their life took a turn for the worse. What do you do?

You are in need of a financial miracle. You have asked God to provide based on His Word. Your heart is confident. You believed that you received when you prayed, but you lose your job or you're hit with a judgment of some kind. Things have only gotten worse. What do you do?

These can, without question, be tough times, but whenever we make the choice to release our faith, there is going to be something that comes to challenge us. Its goal is to make us feel like our prayers and faith didn't work. We can *never* confirm the dependability of God's Word or the validity of faith on the circumstances of this world. The Word and faith are solid spiritual forces that are not predicated on anything but the character of God.

When you choose to walk by faith, you can't be moved by the sudden shifting of this external world. We are commanded in 2 Corinthians 4:18 not to look at the things we can see because they are temporary. We are commanded to look at the things we cannot see because they are eternal. To be successful at walking and living by faith, you have to keep your eyes on the Word of God, or you'll be blown away. The storms of life are coming, and there is no way around them. It's a part of this natural life. But when the conditions around you change, instead of changing with them, tighten your belt of faith and dig deeper into the Word of God. Don't put your eyes on the natural, but keep them on the supernatural. Winds can be blowing all around you, trees flying and houses collapsing, but if you keep your eyes on the unseen realm (the realm where God dwells), the hairs on your head won't even be moved.

So when the report gets worse, just believe God! When it looks like the situation goes the wrong way after you prayed, just believe God! We walk by faith and not by sight (2 Corinthians 5:7). The external circumstances *don't move us!* In Acts 20:22–24, it was revealed to Paul by the Holy Spirit that he was going to suffer affliction. Paul was obeying God, and yet the Holy Spirit warned him that affliction was coming. Here is what Paul said: "None of these things move me." And they can't move you, either! Get your feet solid on the rock of the Word of God so when the storms of life come, they won't blow you away. You're not alone. God is with you! He loves you and He wants you to stand your ground. So no matter what the report is, just believe God!

Today's Scriptures: 2 Corinthians 4:18; 2 Corinthians 5:7; Acts 20:22–24.

Today's Prayer/Confession: No matter what happens around me, I will not be moved. I'm strong in the Lord and in the power of His might. My faith is working and my position is strong. I believe God!

Get Out of the Box!

There was a time when I was so timid I wouldn't step out to do anything. I knew I had a call on my life, but I wouldn't talk in front of people out of fear of saying the wrong thing. The thought of standing before people would have me sick to my stomach for days, so consequently I did my best to stay in the background. As I got older, I could see the impact that fear was having on my life. There were things that I wanted to accomplish but had not been able to. I knew there had to be change or I would run the risk of forfeiting the plan of God for my life.

If we are not watchful, we can take the God-sized vision within us and ignore it or shrink it down to something small because of fear. Fear is a spirit whose mission is to stop us from moving forward. It cripples and boxes us in so we never accomplish what God has purposed for our advancement in life.

Many years ago, I heard the story of a man named B.P., who was born in the early 1900s with polio. The disease left him crippled. B.P. grew in size, and his mother could no longer carry him around, so she made a sturdy wooden box and placed the child in it. She would drag him around the house in the box while she tended to her daily tasks. Every so often, she would see B.P. rocking the box back and forth until he tipped it over in an attempt to free himself. When his mother saw this, she would immediately yell, "B.P., you get back in that box!" Out of obedience, B.P. would scoot back into the box. He continued this practice as he got older, and his mother continued yelling, "B.P., get back in that box!"

But B.P. said, "One day I'm going to get out of this box. I may be in it on the outside, but I'm out on the inside!"

Fear is like B.P.'s mother. It yells, "Stay on that job. Don't you dare try to launch your own business!" "Don't step out. What if you fail?" "You're not as smart as the others!" "You don't have what it takes!" "You don't have a degree!" "It will never work for you like it did them." "Get back in the box!"

The box represents a place of confinement and for many that is a place of comfort. But we have to have the same determination as B.P. and say, "I'm getting out of this box. I may be in on the outside, but one day I'm getting out because I'm out on the inside!" B.P. did get out of the box and became a great scientist.

What has God told you to do that fear is telling you that you can't? Fear is a liar. It has its origin in Satan, who is revealed in John 8:44 as the "father of lies." Anything God has placed in your heart can and will be done *if* you step out of the box of fear. We are told in 2 Timothy 1:7: *"For God has not given us a spirit of fear, but of power and of love and of a sound mind."* If God didn't give fear to us, we don't have to accept it or hold on to it. You have been given a spirit of power, which is strength and ability. You have been given the spirit of love, which, based on 1 Corinthians 13:8, will never fail. And finally, you have the spirit of a sound mind, which is self-control. You can do it! God has given you the control, strength, and ability, and because of His love, you won't fail. How can you lose? Obey God! Get out of the box and take the plunge.

Have a fearless day!

Today's Scriptures: John 8:44; 2 Timothy 1:7; 1 Corinthians 13:8.

Today's Prayer/Confession: Father, I thank you that fear has no place in me. I have the spirit of power, love, and a sound mind, and I can do all things through you, because you have given me the strength!

A Living Vessel

Former British hostage Terry Waite was captured in 1987 and held for five years in Lebanon. I remember watching an interview with Barbara Walters after his release in 1991. While in custody, the only book Mr. Waite was allowed to read was a King James Version of the Bible. Imagine being in solitary confinement for five years with nothing but the Word of God. Mr. Waite told Barbara Walters, "As I continued to read the Bible, the words on the pages came alive."

Those words have stuck with me for all these years. I thought about Hebrews 4:12 (NIV): *"For the word of God is living and active. Sharper than any double-edged sword, it penetrates even to dividing soul and spirit, joints and marrow; it judges the thoughts and attitudes of the heart."* What Terry Waite did for five years was feed and build his spirit on the Word of God. He had no additional outside influences and was able to use the Word of God to eventually get himself out of captivity. We have to understand that the Word of God is more than a sleep aide—it is the life and breath of God. It moves and transforms. It is not dead, dry, or dull.

Your spirit has the capacity to carry the Word of God. It took the place of the Ark of the Covenant from the days of old. The Ark was a vessel that housed the tablets of stone with the Ten Commandments of God. It was a sacred vessel, just like your human spirit. It's not only the place for the Word of God, but it's also the place that God himself has chosen to dwell.

"And I will put my spirit within you, and cause you to walk in my statutes, and ye shall keep my judgments, and do them" (Ezekiel 36:27).

If you are a believer, you are a carrier for the living Word of God. This is why it is so important to handle your vessel in a holy manner. When the children of Israel or other nations mishandled the Ark of the Covenant, it cost someone his life. It's time for us to begin to recognize our true value and worth as vessels of God. When the world touches the "Ark" of our lives, we should be so full of the life of God that the darkness in them has no choice but to flee.

Wherever the Ark of the Covenant was, that place was blessed. In 2 Samuel 6:9–14, we read the account of King David recovering the Ark from the home of a man named Obed-Edom. The Bible says that Obed-

Edom's entire household was blessed because the Ark was there. The same applies to you. God told Abraham that we would be blessed, but we would also be a blessing. Because we are the vessels of God, everywhere we go is blessed. Deuteronomy 28:6 says we are blessed going in and blessed going out. Why? Because we are the carriers of God.

Today as you step out, remember the treasure that you are. You are a living, breathing representation of the Ark of God!

Have a great day!

Today's Scriptures: Hebrews 4:12; Ezekiel 36:27; 2 Samuel 6:9–14; Deuteronomy 28:6.

Today's Prayer/Confession: Father, thank you for making me a living vessel—one that you have poured yourself into. Help me to live conscious of who I am as a carrier of the living Word of God. In Jesus's name, Amen!

A Righteousness Consciousness

I was ten when I accepted Jesus as my Savior. I remember it just as if it happened yesterday. It was a Friday night in downtown Milwaukee at a citywide crusade for Christ. I was so excited about my new life that I danced and cried about it the entire weekend. I read my Bible and prayed as best I could, and the joy of the Lord was all over me. I laughed and sang old hymns I had learned going to church with my grandmother. I was good! Life was good!

Monday rolled around and I had to go back to school. Recess time came and I was standing on the playground with my friends when suddenly I heard an eruption of vulgar language. Before I knew it, I yelled out, "I'm saved, and I'm not supposed to be talking like this!" and slapped my hand over my mouth. Yep, it was me. After all the singing, dancing, and giving praise to God, it took one walk to the playground to deflate my spiritual bubble. It bothered me so terribly that I moped for days, thinking about the words I had spoken and the fact that I was supposed to be a Christian. In my mind, I had blown it.

When I was growing up, my mother had a spiritual mentor named Alpha who lived in another state. When mom would face life's challenges, she would call Alpha, so I asked my mother to give me Alpha's number. I didn't tell her why, because I was too embarrassed to tell anyone else. So when I had a moment of privacy, I slipped off into a room and made the call. I will never forget her words, and this is what she said, "Melva, the position you hold with God is not easily taken or shaken. It would take more than just a few curse words to stop God from loving you. In fact, He never will. Your place as a son of God is secure because of what Jesus did for you. What you are dealing with right now is a sin consciousness. You are more conscious of the mistake you made than of the righteous person that you are. 1 John 1:9 is there for you. Use it, forgive yourself, and move on." I was freed that day.

When we make mistakes, we cannot keep our eyes on the wrong we have done, or we will never advance in our walk with Christ. When we ask God to forgive us and truly repent (go in a different direction), God doesn't remember what we have done (Psalms 103:12). We continually put our mistakes in front of Him, and every time we do, we can hear Him say, "I don't know what you are talking about. I don't remember any sin that you have committed. It has all been covered in the blood of Jesus Christ."

There are too many Christians walking back to the world because they are too conscious of the mistakes they have made. They simply struggle to forgive themselves. Whether you struggle to believe it or not, you are forgiven. You are the righteousness of God in Christ Jesus. If you begin thinking about the righteousness that you have been made to be, your life will conform to what you behold. On the other hand, if you keep sin before your eyes, you will continue to walk in it because you're more conscious of it.

Stay in the Word of God! Think righteous, act righteous, and if you make a mistake, repent, shake the dust off your feet and keep serving God. Jesus is sitting at God's right hand as our intercessor. When the accuser comes before the Father telling Him what we have done wrong, Jesus lovingly turns to the Father and says, "I died for that. Every sin and mistake is covered. Father, you promised to apply my blood and forgive them. You can't hold it against them. They are free!"

God is not holding your mistake against you. Don't hold it against yourself. Live with a righteousness consciousness, and mistakes you make will begin to diminish.

Have a righteous day!

Today's Scriptures: 1 John 1:9; Psalms 103:12; 2 Corinthians 5:21.

Today's Prayer/Confession: Father, 2 Corinthians 5:21 states that you made Jesus to be sin for me. He knew no sin, but He did it so that I might be made your righteousness in Him. I don't have to live with a sin consciousness because you have redeemed me from the curse of sin. I'm free today because of the price that Jesus paid! Thank you for this, in Jesus's name, Amen!

Get Out There and Do It!

There seems to be a great deal of insecurity in the world today—individuals looking for their sense of worth and value in other people, things, and positions. You can't live the God kind of life if your sense of value is predicated on something or in anyone other than God. It's locked in Him and Him alone. If you were like Job and lost everything you owned, including those you loved, would you lose yourself? Would you still be complete and whole, or would your life become meaningless? Don't misunderstand me. I know that there is a very real time of grief associated with loss, but the person God created you to be in the midst of that loss should never budge.

Insecurities come when we have failed to consistently see ourselves as God has created us to be. He would never have sacrificed His only begotten Son for an individual who was worthless. David in Psalms 139:14 says that we are *"fearfully and wonderfully made."* That means you were made in awe, with honor and respect. You are priceless because the God of heaven created you, and not only that, He placed Himself in you through His Spirit. Think about that. Would our Holy, all-powerful God choose to live in a worthless vessel? I think not. It's time to change the way you think. You have to see yourself as God does!

God wants you to experience all the blessings there are in *this* life. My grandmother, affectionately known as "Mamma," is eighty-seven years old, and although she has lived a good, godly life, she didn't even scratch the surface of the blessings of God, and it was because of the way she saw herself. She struggled with her own worth. Because she came up in the south during the times of segregation, she never expected to have much in life. She knew she was loved by God and dedicated her entire life to Him, but she settled. I don't fault her, because she was never told that she was more than just a cook. So that's where she found her worth, in her ability to cook. She wouldn't go beyond her own self-image. But there is so much more in my grandmother.

Don't allow a poor self-image to hold you back in life. There's a whole world out here to harness. Don't delay because you are waiting for someone else to give you the green light. God gave it to you a long time ago. What are you waiting for? I certainly hope you are not waiting for people. If you wait for others to validate you, you'll be waiting for the rest of your life. You're good, and you've got the goods. God made you, and He has equipped you with everything you need that pertains to life and godliness (2 Peter 1:3). Get out there and do it!

Today's Scriptures: Psalms 139:14; 2 Peter 1:3.

Today's Prayer/Confession: I am fearfully and wonderfully made because I was made in the image and likeness of God. I am valuable to Him, and He has equipped me with everything I need to be a success in this life. I will not wait for the approval of man when God has given me His plan. I'm good because I'm God's!

Choose Life!

One morning I woke to attend 5 a.m. prayer at our local church. I opened my eyes in more than enough time, but a thought came, convincing me that I was too tired and needed to rest. It was my flesh. My spirit was pulling me to get up, but my body didn't want to move. Voices were going back and forth inside of me: "Get up, there are things you need to pray out. God knows you're tired. Your body needs the extra rest." And on and on it went. When it was all over, it was 6:33 a.m., and time for me to start the day. I had wasted almost two hours listening to the inner battle between my flesh and my spirit, and in the end my flesh won. Ugghh!

Over the years, I've learned that the person who is stronger isn't always the winner, especially when it comes to the battle between the flesh and the spirit. In this battle, the winner is determined by the voice acted on and obeyed. My spirit may be strong, but if I listen to the voice of my flesh, the strength of my spirit is irrelevant. Adam was strong and full of authority when God created him, but he listened to the voice of a dethroned spirit and lost it all. On that same turn, individuals can be spiritually weak, but if they listen to the voice of God through their own spirits, they will achieve victory in life. Romans 6:16 (NLT) says: *"Don't you realize that whatever you choose to obey becomes your master?"* When I obey the voice of the flesh, I enslave myself to his mastery, but when I obey the voice of my spirit, I live freely as a son.

We were created and redeemed to live as sons, not slaves. When we listen to the voice of our human spirits influenced by the Holy Spirit, He can be trusted to handle us like the sons we are. But the flesh won't because its influencing voice is Satan. You can be faithful to obey the dictates of your flesh, but all you will ever gain is death. There will be satisfaction and pleasure along the way, but the end of the road is going to lead to death (Galatians 6:7–8). Satan has nothing good to reward you with because there is no good thing in him. He's a thief, murderer, and destroyer (John 10:10), and that is all he has for your acts of obedience to the flesh. Obeying the dictates of the Holy Spirit will lead you to life and peace. So the choice is always yours.

I love what God said in Deuteronomy 30:19: *"I have set before you life and death, blessing and cursing, therefore, CHOOSE LIFE."* He not only told us what He placed before us, He also told us what to choose. Let's do it! Choose Life!

If you've been like me and you have been listening to the voice of your flesh, don't get under condemnation. It is behind us. Tomorrow is a new day, and God's mercies are with us. Although we missed it today, we won't tomorrow. We choose life!

Have a great day!

Today's Scriptures: Romans 6:16; Galatians 6:7–8; John 10:10; Deuteronomy 30:19.

Today's Prayer/Confession: Father, thank you for giving me the power to choose. I'm determined to obey the voice of my spirit because it is influenced by your Holy Spirit. In Jesus's name, Amen!

The Aged—A Crown of Wisdom

This weekend I had the honored privilege of spending a few hours sitting at the feet of an individual who has been walking with God for more than fifty-three years. I call her a General. Her walk has been much like those you find in the Old Testament, and her very being dripped with the presence of God. It reminded me of Enoch. *"Enoch walked with God. Then he couldn't be found, because God took him from this life"* (Genesis 5:24 NIRV).

There is a godly generation about to transition from the earth—those who will leave with their wisdom and spiritual experiences. Their spiritual wealth is necessary for the generations that will follow them. It's locked in their bellies, and if we are not watchful, they will go home without relinquishing what they have. But do we want to hear? Do we really desire to know where they have been or what it was like to walk with God as Adam did in the cool of the day? I certainly want to know, and God wants you to know.

Imagine what many of us would be like if our mentors and leaders were those whom God used to part Red Seas or conquer fortified cities by shouting praises unto Him. Whether you believe it or not, they still exist today, and many are right under your nose. If you look for someone of great stature—someone who may look the part—you will miss them. Those who walk with God look just like you and me. Their skin color is irrelevant, because all you can see is the glory of God. They may be no one special to those on the earth, but they are powerfully great in God. We need what they possess.

I love the stories my grandmother tells. I've heard them a thousand times, but every time she tells them, I listen and laugh or cry as if it were my first time hearing. There is so much in those who are older than we are, and we want to learn to squeeze them until they are dry. God is in the aged. They know Him. They have seen Him. They've walked with Him. So don't close your ears. Listen and you will hear God speak to your heart.

"The counsel of the LORD standeth for ever, the thoughts of His heart to all generations" (Psalms 33:11).

Have a blessed day!

Today's Scriptures: Genesis 5:24; Psalms 33:11.

Today's Prayer/Confession: I purpose in my heart to receive the word of the wise. I will keep my heart open to hear what they have to say. God is with the aged, and His wisdom is their crown.

Zoe: The God Kind of Life

We only get one life, so it makes sense to do our best to live it to the fullest. God has a divine plan for us, so living life to the fullest means being what God wants us to be, doing what God wants us to do, and going where God wants us to go.

Your natural mind cannot imagine the blessings that God has in store. They are just waiting for you to appropriate (receive) them. God wants your life to be complete and whole with nothing missing, nothing lacking or broken. I realize for many this may seem to be a fairytale life—something unimaginable or unattainable—a pipe dream. But based on the Word of God, it's not.

There is a Hebrew word that reveals the life God wants you to have. That word is *Zoe*. Zoe is the God-quality of life. It's the life that Jesus revealed to us in John 10:10: *"But I have come that they might have life (Zoe) and have life (Zoe) in abundance."* Zoe is God manifesting Himself in and through our lives. It's impossible to have it and others not to see it.

The Zoe life is the good life. It's a life that is independent of man, yet totally dependent upon God (Philippians 4:19). It's having all of your needs met—spiritual, physical, and material. Zoe will have everyone in your household serving God, and those who don't will soon be in the process of coming to know Him. Zoe puts money in your bank account, health in your body, and peace in your mind. The Zoe life thrives in the positive and steers clear of the negative. It believes the best about every person (1 Corinthians 13:7 Amplified) and positions you to prosper wherever you go.

Don't you want this type of life? If you are a believer, you already have it! Zoe comes when Christ comes into our lives. He *is* Zoe, and when we allow Him to live through us, we experience life, in abundance, to the full until it overflows.

Have a great day!

Today's Scriptures: John 10:10; Philippians 4:19; 1 Corinthians 13:7.

Today's Prayer/Confession: Father, thank you for imparting to me the Zoe life—your quality of life. I purpose in my heart to be an example of an individual whom you have blessed and acknowledge that my life is a channel of blessing to others. Thank you for this! In Jesus's name, Amen!

154

I Will Not Remove Mine Integrity

"God forbid that I should justify you: till I die I will not remove mine integrity from me" (Job 27:5).

The word *integrity* is a very powerful word. Unfortunately, these days it is rarely at the top of the list of group discussions. In the dictionary, integrity is defined as "adherence to moral and ethical principles; soundness of moral character." To sum it up, integrity is simply honesty of character. In Hebrew it's the transliterated word *Tom*, pronounced *Tome,* it means "simplicity, to be upright, complete, and full." So the obvious opposites would be "complicated, leaning, incomplete, and empty."

As Christians, it is our responsibility to constantly examine ourselves, ensuring that what we see is in compliance with the Word of God. If there are areas in which we fall short, we have to be willing to make the necessary adjustments, bringing our life into subjection to the Word of God. If we don't, our character will bend toward doing things in a leaning, compromising way. Whenever you find people who have complicated or depleted lives, meaning they always seem to come up short, the integrity issue is usually the root of the problem. Their inability to pay the rent or stay out of trouble is the fruit, but the lack of integrity is the root.

What we should desire is the fruit of our lives producing abundance in every way, because the root of our lives is founded on the integrity of the Word of God. There is no room for compromise, and any place in us that has a slight bend to err, cover, mishandle, or misappropriate, has to be exposed and checked immediately or it will grow into a tree with integrity issues.

On my birthday a few years ago, I wanted to be a blessing to a group of ladies in our church, so I took them to a little boutique. I decided that I would buy a purse for each of the ladies. Our group was large, and each of them wanted to get additional items that they would pay for themselves. By the time I reached the counter, the clerk was extremely flustered. Being a new store, they hadn't served this many people at one time. I immediately knew something was wrong when the young woman gave me my total. I thought to myself, "Either they are giving items away or she has made a gross error."

Once she completed my sale, I quickly moved out of the way, giving place to the other individuals in line. I knew the young clerk must have failed to ring up several of the items I had purchased. The entire time my flesh was saying, "Walk out of the store. Read the receipt after you leave." The store was miles away from my home, so going back wasn't an option on that particular day. Although I was verbally silent, the idea of gaining so much "loot" really excited me. No one knew but me. My mind started thinking, "Oh, the blessing of the Lord has made me rich!" But in reality it had not. This was a mistake that could have potentially cost this young woman her job.

God was watching me, so right in the middle of the store, I said, "I think we made a mistake. I must have missed giving you some of my items." In my flesh I felt this deflation and almost started to cry, but integrity wouldn't allow me to steal from the store. It placed a fort around me. Was I tempted? Are you kidding me? Of course, I was. Spirit-filled, Bible teacher, pastor, and all, but the integrity of my heart wouldn't let me. There was too much at stake. I couldn't walk out of the store.

Integrity is being a person of strong moral character inwardly and then acting on it outwardly—seen or unseen. Integrity is about you. It's how you choose to live your own life. When you choose to walk in integrity, it will:

Preserve you—Psalms 25:21

Stop you from sliding—Psalms 26:1

Redeem & extend mercy to you—Psalms 26:11

Skillfully guide you by the hand of God—Psalms 78:72

Set you before the face of God forever—Psalms 41:12

You won't miss anything when you choose to be a person of integrity. It's speaking, thinking, and doing what is right because it's right to do. Have a great day!

Today's Scriptures: Job 27:5; Psalms 25:21, 26:1, 26:11, 78:72, 41:12.

Today's Prayer/Confession: Today I choose to walk in my integrity. I will operate in truth in my thoughts, actions, and words. I will do what is right in the sight of God and man, in private as well as public. In Jesus's name, Amen!

Be Okay With You

I had just picked up my twins from elementary school when from the back seat my son, Quenton, asks for the definition of a particular word. I actually hadn't heard the word before and didn't have the answer, so I said to him, "Quenton, I have no idea what that word means."

He replied, "You don't? You don't know what it means? If you don't know what this word means, then you are not as smart as I thought you were." Thud, cricket, cricket ...

I kept driving and looking straight ahead, but his words were ringing in my head and eating at my heart. "You're not as smart as I thought you were. You're not as smart as I thought you were." That was more than twenty years ago, and I still remember it as if it happened this morning. Quenton meant no harm. He wasn't being disrespectful. He thought I knew everything, but he realized that day that I didn't—and thank God.

It's too much pressure to leave people with the idea that you are the guru in life. What Quenton saw was my limitations, and although his revelation came in a way that was uncomfortable for me, I didn't run away from the moment. After several minutes of silence, I finally spoke up and said, "You are right. I don't know everything, but I do know where to go to get the information I need. Quenton, it's not important to know everything, but recognizing that you have access to all that you need is important." His response was, "Okay," and for him, that was it.

Although Quenton's words hung with me, they were a child-like reminder that I wasn't "all that." It's so important that we learn to be okay with ourselves and never live endeavoring to impress other people or making people think that we are infallible. I could have defended myself, but the truth was I didn't know everything, and had I tried to prove that I did, I would have lost credibility with my son. Leave room for your humanity. Jesus did. He never sinned, but he did constantly say, "It's the Father in me that's doing the work."

We are God's workmanship (Ephesians 2:10), which means we are a work in progress. He's still working on us. So don't put more pressure on yourself if you don't think you measure up. Jesus is our standard. He is the only one we are required to measure up to, and because of God's grace, we already do. Be okay being you. If there are areas that need to change, use the Word to transform your thinking and change. It's very simple. You are not flawless. You are in the process of maturing and growing into all that God has ordained you to be.

Much love toward you today, God bless you.

Today's Scriptures: Ephesians 2:10.

Today's Prayer/Confession: Father, I know that I am a work in progress. I will endeavor to cover myself in your Word and allow you to bring to light the areas that need to be changed and transformed in my life. Thank you for not requiring perfection but for pouring out grace as I move toward maturity in Christ. In Jesus's name, Amen!

He's a Father to the Fatherless

One day, in an act of self-pity, I was having a meltdown in the company of my husband. I "felt" like all the authoritative men in my life had in one way or another left or abandoned me. My husband listened in silence, and being the loving person he is, leaned over and kissed me on the cheek. My husband learned many years ago not to respond during those times. The longing in my heart was bigger than he could handle.

Realizing that all my emotional stuff was in vain, I rolled over and finally fell asleep. When I opened my eyes the next morning this is what I heard: *"I'm making you. I'm investing in you. I'm making you a child after my own heart. Don't look to natural people to make you what you ought to be. You are a work in my own hands. I've got you and it's my job to be your Father and not a mere man's."* His voice was authoritative and strong and I knew it was the voice of God.

I spent a great deal of my young life longing for a father, one who would love and embrace me, imparting to me wisdom for life. One day as I was studying the scriptures, I came across Psalms 68:4–6 and my life changed forever:

Sing to God, sing praise to his name, extol him who rides on the clouds his name is the LORD and rejoice before him. ***A Father to the fatherless, a defender of widows,*** *is God in his holy dwelling.* ***God sets the lonely in families,*** *he leads forth the prisoners with singing; but the rebellious live in a sun-scorched land.* (Psalms 68:4-6 NIV)

A Father to the fatherless! That's what I needed ... my very own father. I realized that this particular scripture was not talking about a man. This scripture was talking about God. He's the Father to the fatherless. But learning to accept His fatherhood wasn't an easy thing for me to do. I wasn't accustomed to having a father genuinely interested in my life, someone who thought about me all the time. But God does. In fact, in Isaiah 49:16 He said that He engraved my life upon the palms of His hands, and the walls of my life are continually before Him.

If you're like I was and find yourself longing for a father, mentor, or investor, God is the one. There's something so sweet about having Him as your father. He completes you, He makes you feel good about yourself, and He's with you everywhere you go. In His eyes you are the greatest.

He accepts you the way you are, but He loves you too much to leave you that way. He fills your life with good things, and when you get older, He renews your youth like the eagles. He walks with you, talks with you, and protects you from predators and enemies. He comforts you in times of pain and loneliness and fills you with His very own strength. He's a friend who sticks closer than a brother. Jesus called Him the Father of whom all fatherhood derives their name. There is no father like The Father. He's Abba, dear Daddy, the one who loves us all.

I could go on and on, but I'll close with this: Thank you, Father God, for being here for me and all those in the world like me. We love you!

Today's Scriptures: Psalms 68:4–6; Isaiah 49:16.

Not One Day Longer in the Wilderness

In the book of Numbers we read the account of the children of Israel's journey from Egypt through the wilderness to the land of Canaan, better known as The Promised Land. Moses, their leader, told them God was going to deliver them out of the hands of the Egyptians. They were excited to go because the land promised was described as "a land flowing with milk and honey."

Little did Moses or the children of Israel know that the journey, which should have taken them anywhere from eleven to thirty days, would take them forty years. This route can now be flown in as little as two hours. As you can see, the distance wasn't very long. Imagine planning a vacation to Hawaii. You leave on April 19, 2011 and don't arrive until April 19, 2051. That's just too long.

There was one thing that not only stopped the progress of their journey, but also caused many to die in the wilderness—complaining. If you read Numbers chapters 11 through 17, it gives account after account of their various complaints and this was the result:

Then the LORD said to Moses and Aaron, "How long will this wicked nation complain about me? I have heard everything the Israelites have been saying. Now tell them this: 'As surely as I live, I will do to you the very things I heard you say. I, the LORD, have spoken! You will all die here in this wilderness! Because you complained against me, none of you who are twenty years old or older and were counted in the census will enter the land I swore to give you. The only exceptions will be Caleb son of Jephunneh and Joshua son of Nun. You said your children would be taken captive. Well, I will bring them safely into the land, and they will enjoy what you have despised. But as for you, your dead bodies will fall in this wilderness. And your children will be like shepherds, wandering in the wilderness forty years. In this way, they will pay for your faithlessness, until the last of you lies dead in the wilderness. Because the men who explored the land were there for forty days, you must wander in the wilderness for forty years—a year for each day, suffering the consequences of your sins. You will discover what it is like to have me for an enemy. I, the LORD, have spoken! I will do these things to every member of the community who has conspired against me. They will all die here in this wilderness!" (Numbers 14:26–35 NLT)

Not good. Not good at all. These accounts, as well as others, were recorded to be an example to us. God wanted us to see the results of complaining. Those who complained never made it into the land that was promised to them. They died in the wilderness. When we choose to complain, we may experience trickles of blessings here and there, but we will never *live* in the place God has for us. God doesn't want us to just experience a promise or two every now and then. He wants our lives to be housed in the land of His promises. He doesn't want us to just get healed; He wants us living in divine health. He doesn't want us to just have our needs supplied; He wants our cup to run over with His blessings at all times. But complaining will hinder our advancement to God's place of abundance.

Every time God or Moses became angry with the children of Israel, it was because of the complaints of their mouths. They said it was too hard or that the way they lived in the past was better than what they currently had. But the reality was that in the past they were beaten and had lived as slaves. Their continual complaining clouded their ability to recall God's hand of provision. They forgot He had delivered them out of the hands of their enemy, parted the Red Sea, baked their bread with His own hands, and flew fresh meat in every single day. God was so good to them! Their children wore the same pairs of shoes for forty years, but the shoes never wore out. Their feet grew and the shoes grew with their feet. What did they have to complain about?

What do we really have to complain about? God has been good to us, also. He has made ways when there was no way, and He has opened doors that men said would never be opened. He has loved us in spite of how we acted and never even thought about abandoning us. What is there to complain about? It doesn't matter what is going on in life. Philippians 2:14 (NIV) says *"Do* everything *without complaining or arguing."* Let's obey the Word of God and not walk through the wilderness one day longer!

God bless you! Have a complaint-free day!

Today's Scriptures: Numbers Chapters 11–17; Philippians 2:14.

Today's Prayer/Confession: Father, in the name of Jesus, I commit to you that I will stop complaining. I want the promises of God continually flowing in my life. Help me to keep a guard over my mouth, attitude, and thinking. I can do this because your power within me is strong and I thank you for it. In Jesus's name, Amen!

Just Go!

I was recently at the home-going service of a sister in Christ who had passed suddenly, leaving a husband and three children. At the conclusion of the service, the family was escorted down the center aisle and out the doors of the church. There was a lady standing directly in front of me who must have been a close friend of the family because as they passed by, a little eight-year-old figure leaned out of the center aisle into the pews saying to her, "Did you see my mommy? She's in there." She was pointing to the casket.

A cloak of prayer came over me and tears rolled down my cheeks as I thought about all of the children around the world who may have lost their mothers at an early age. My mind went to a very close friend who had been the same age when she lost her mother. With my friend in mind, I began to pray for God's grace on and within this little girl. I asked Him to surround her with individuals who would love and train her in the ways of God, teaching her of her covenant rights in Christ. I asked God to fill the huge void that she will one day feel as the reality of the loss of her mother settles in. I prayed for the call of God on her and asked Him to cover and protect her all the days of her life. When I finished, I had a release in my heart. My mission was accomplished and I could go home.

God will send us to places to impact lives in unimaginable ways. My husband and I rode fourteen hours to attend this funeral because I had this deep sense *to go*. We were there to support a close friend, but in my heart I know for certain that God sent me to pray for the life of that little girl.

We were told in 1 Corinthians 6:20 that we were bought with a price and our life is not our own. God needs us to be available for Him to use. He desires to reach through us in order to touch lives, and He wants to be able to do it at any given time and in any place. We are His hands and feet. When we are willing to go, we position God to move in the lives of His people, and because He loves us so much, He is always looking for ways to reach us. And He will do it in unconventional ways.

When I packed my bag to leave the day before the funeral, all I had in my heart was *Go*. So out of obedience I went. We have to be willing to listen to the still, small voice of the Lord in our lives. You never know who needs you. Throughout the course of your day, look for opportunities to invest in someone else. Don't let the hustle and bustle of life weaken your sensitivity. People are depending on us. Let's not let them down. Who knows where that little girl is going to go in life? God knows, and it's going to be good!

Have a great day and just go!

Today's Scripture: 1 Corinthians 6:20.

Today's Prayer/Confession: Father, today I commit to living sensitive to your Spirit. I desire to go where you tell me and speak what you tell me to speak. Make my life a vessel you can use to bring glory to your name. Help me to obey the leading and prompting of the Holy Spirit so you can touch lives, no matter how small, on the earth. In Jesus's name, Amen!

The Faith Fight!

Walking by faith is no cake walk. It's not for the faint of heart. When we choose to step out and trust God, no matter what the arena is, we have to be firm and fixed in our belief or the first punch from our challenger will knock us out of the ring.

I've learned that we as individuals are not necessarily the focus of Satan's attention, but he's definitely got his eyes on our faith. He's okay when our faith is weak, little, or inactive, but when our faith stands in front of him asking, "Who are you to defy the God of Israel?" it makes the enemy nervous and the heat is on.

"Fight the good fight of faith" (1 Timothy 6:12). It's called the good fight because the fight has been fixed and we are supposed to always win and never lose. Yes, it's going to get rough, but it's still a good fight. You'll find people in the Body of Christ running, complaining, and trying to weasel their way out of the battle, but you cannot run, cover your face, or fold up in the fetal position. In contending for your faith, you will have to stand your ground and fight!

Don't allow the enemy, through circumstances, to keep punching you without retaliation. When you're getting hit and you're not hitting back, it's called "a beat-down scene." God didn't give you His Spirit, His Word, or faith to sit back and watch you get beat down. So the fight officially begins when you're hit and you start hitting back. That's when it's on!

When I was about eight years old, I was bullied by a girl in elementary school. One day after school, she physically attacked me, and since I wasn't a fighter, this scene wasn't favorable for me. Someone quickly ran to get my twin brother. It was midwinter and quite cold, so when my brother arrived on the scene, with his hands in his pockets he said, "It's too cold to fight!" He left me on the playground. But something inside of me clicked when he walked off. I became aware that the only one that was going to get that girl off me was me. So I began to swing back, and when I did, the fight ended quickly.

"Use every piece of God's armor to resist the enemy in the time of evil, so that after the battle you will still be standing firm" (Ephesians 6:13 NLT).

In closing, remember that we have been called to this fight, and it's a good one! Have a great day!

Today's Scriptures: 1 Timothy 6:12; Ephesians 6:13.

Today's Prayer/Confession: Father, help me not to shrink back when the blows of the enemy come my way. Give me the grace to endure hardness as a good soldier. I know you have promised victory, so I stand in the face of opposition, knowing you will deliver me out of them all. In Jesus's name, Amen!

Rooted in God

Be not deceived; God is not mocked: for whatsoever a man soweth, that shall he also reap. For he that soweth to his flesh shall of the flesh reap corruption; but he that soweth to the Spirit shall of the Spirit reap life everlasting (Galatians 6:7–8).

Notice two phrases: *"shall of the flesh reap"* and *"shall of the Spirit reap."* The word *of* is the Greek transliterated word *"EK,"* which means "by or from." It is the place from which something originates. So Galatians 6 is saying wherever you sow or scatter is also the place that your harvest is going to originate or flow from. Whether we recognize it or not, every one of us has a daily practice of scattering seed. It could be time seed, attention seed, attitude seed, resource seed, or energy seed. Whatever you find yourself doing, acting on or saying is a seed sown. This includes doing nothing. If you do nothing, you will produce nothing.

The important thing to observe is the fact that your harvest is going to come from the places that you have scattered your seed, and if those places don't have the type of inventory you desire to see in your life, then I would advise you to attentively consider where your seed is sown. If you sow into a place that only has sickness, death, marital problems, children on drugs, loneliness, debt, or other woes, the only fruit or harvest it can produce is what it possesses.

We understand how this works in the natural. I personally don't care for brussels sprouts, but I do love watermelon. What would happen if one day, I decide to grow my own vine of watermelons, and instead of planting (sowing) watermelon seeds, I plant (sow) brussels sprout seeds instead. When I see brussels sprouts growing in my garden, it would be silly to get upset with the ground or the seeds for producing the wrong harvest. The ground can only give what it has been given, and the seed can only produce itself. If I want the ground to produce watermelons, I've got to plant watermelon seeds in the ground.

This is why sowing to the Spirit is vital. It is the fertile ground for our life seed. The ground of the Spirit is living ground. It produces an abundance of health, wealth, peace, deliverance, and freedom because that's all it has. Nothing negative or bad can be produced from this ground, because it's rooted in God.

James 1:17 clearly states that every good gift comes down from the Father, so if it's from God, it's good. But you won't experience His goodness if you sow to your flesh. The flesh has nothing good to give you. It can only produce from the place it is rooted, and as the Spirit is rooted in God, so is the flesh rooted in death and that is all it can give. You can be faithful, but all the flesh will ever be able to reward you with is death.

Romans 8:2 states that *"the law of the Spirit of life in Christ Jesus has made me free from the law of sin and death."* Let's sow to the Spirit today and we won't have to deal with the produce of the flesh (Galatians 5:16 NKJV).

Today's Scriptures: Galatians 6:7–8; James 1:17; Romans 8:2; Galatians 5:16.

Today's Prayer/Confession: Father, I choose to walk in the Spirit and not after the dictates of my flesh. My flesh does not control me. I want to produce life and peace in my life, so I scatter my seed in places that produce your life and your peace. In Jesus's name, Amen!

Love the Lord Your God

In Mark 12:30 (NKJV), Jesus said these words, *"Love the Lord your God, with all your heart, with all your soul, with all your mind, and with all your strength."* What does it mean to love God with all my heart, soul, and strength? If we look closely we can recognize that we are being instructed to employ our total being in a love relationship with God.

First, there is the heart, which obviously is not the blood-pumping organ in the human body, but is the abiding place of our God. The heart represents the human spirit—the eternal core of who we are. The heart is the home of God; therefore, love begins in the heart.

Born with sinful natures, we were not capable of loving God at this level on our own. Human love is not strong or consistent enough and is often predicated on how we feel or our current circumstances. It's like the saints of old used to say, "Sometimes up, and sometimes down, sometimes almost level with the ground." That kind of love couldn't love God the way He deserves to be loved, so God gave us His Divine Love to love Him with.

Romans 5:5 states: *"The love of God is shed abroad in our hearts by the Holy Ghost."* The word *abroad* means "gushed out" or "largely distributed." I always thought God poured His love into our hearts to help us become model examples of 1 Corinthians 13, the great love chapter. But as I've meditated on Romans 5:5, I can see His love was shed in our hearts so that we could love Him as well as others. It is the same love, but He is to be loved first.

Loving God with all your heart is an act of commitment and loyalty. When an opportunity to be disloyal to Him presents itself, you count the cost and choose to please Him over yourself or someone else. When you love Him, you don't desire to disobey or cheat on Him, and even if you do, you are quick to repent and restore the relationship. But your love for Him won't allow you to live in a place of sin or stay in a place of disloyalty.

Loving God with all your soul involves the mind, will, and emotions. How do you love God with your mind, your will, and your emotions? Simple! You honor and acknowledge Him before you do anything else or acknowledge anyone else in every situation and circumstance. When you take time to feed on the Word and transform your way of thinking, that is loving God with your mind. When you are willing to lay down your own ideas, directions, and desires in order to follow His, that is loving God with your will. Instead of moving emotionally when you've received bad news, you bring your emotions under the control of the Word of God by remembering and recalling what He has spoken into your life. That is loving God with your emotions. Loving God with all your soul is giving mental credence to God's ways first, showing Him that you revere and honor His way of doing things above your own.

Loving God with all your strength means that you are willing to engage your natural abilities for His purpose and His cause. It's recognizing Him as Lord of your life, submitting all you are and all you have to advance His will on the earth. It's placing your gifts, talents, and abilities at His disposal and being willing to govern your life as He directs.

Every day is an opportunity for you to love the Lord your God with all your heart, soul, and strength. Loving God is rewarded in ways you can't even imagine—in this life and in the life that is to come.

Have a wonderful day!

Today's Scripture: Mark 12:30; Romans 5:5; 1 Corinthians 13.

Today's Prayer/Confession: Today, I allow myself the privilege of loving God with every fiber of my being. I submit my ways, my thoughts, and my desires to His. As I do this, His Love is positioning me for greatness in life!

Glory to Glory

When I first gave my heart to Jesus, it was the most exciting thing that ever happened to me. I remember the fire and passion of those years and longing for more of Him in my life. I was thrilled to be in church whenever the doors were opened, and even though I was only ten, I kept myself around individuals who had a love and passion for Christ.

Somewhere along the way, things started to change, and what had once been exciting and fresh became mundane and routine. I slowly began to notice old habits creeping back into my life, and being in church wasn't as exciting as it previously had been. That is, until a visiting evangelist came. The evangelist ministered under a strong anointing and helped restart my fire again. That time of ministry got me back on track for a season, but before long I was back in that humdrum place, and I wouldn't come out of it until another "fire wave" hit our church. Those services became "spiritual IVs" that I would live and depend on for many years. Although it helped keep my relationship with God intact, it did not help it grow, and I lived a very carnal, frustrated Christian life.

I know this is a familiar place to many. As pastors, my husband and I have the opportunity to hear the voices of many. A reverberating statement common among parishioners is: "I just don't have the fire I once had, and I'm not growing in my walk with Christ," or "I'm just not being fed in my church anymore."

These types of statements point to our own need to keep the fire of God burning in our lives. Although we are passionate about God, passion alone is not enough to keep us moving in our personal relationship with Christ. It may give our walk a "jump start," but it will not maintain it. People tend to grow weary and begin to coast in their relationship with Christ, because it takes discipline and effort.

I was in and out and always needed an outside source to fuel my spiritual fire, because I was never trained to do it myself. I didn't know that I needed to pray daily and feed my spirit. At that time, no one told me about the importance of confessing and meditating on the Word of God. I thought it was the responsibility of my pastor and the evangelists who came through. I was wrong. When I learned about my responsibility to keep a daily life before God, everything changed. And I started growing and going from glory to glory.

"But we all, with open face beholding as in a glass the glory of the Lord, are changed into the same image from glory to glory, even as by the Spirit of the Lord" (2 Corinthians 3:18).

Every day in Christ should be a day of refreshing and newness. It should never be dull and lifeless. If you are struggling to maintain your spiritual place, you can change that today. God wants you to go from one degree of His glory to the next in your walk with Him. Glory is the excellent brightness of God's presence. God wants His power and presence in such a degree in your life that it manifests itself through you. All it takes is daily discipline and determination.

Go for the gusto! Don't let the fire in you die! Contend for the glory! It may start out rough, but keep at it, and eventually your desires will turn to what you are contending for, and the fire of God will rest upon you as never before. Have a Great Day!

Today's Scripture: 2 Corinthians 3:18.

Today's Prayer/Confession: Every day I commit myself to times of prayer and studying the Word of God, and as a result, the fire of God will rest upon me for the rest of my life!

Christ Is Our Standard

It's important for us to remember that man cannot be the standard for our lives. We can certainly learn and be motivated by others, but we are never to gauge our lives on the actions, opinions, or title of someone else. Our lives must be gauged and governed by the Word of God alone. This is especially true in the church.

We have so many people living with "church hurts"—wounded by their pastors, church members, or spiritual leaders—because they placed more confidence in a person than they did in God. Now don't get me wrong. We are to honor, obey, and respect our leaders based on God's Word, however, our reverence must come with boundaries and a balanced understanding from the Word of God. We can never forget that although called and anointed, people are still flesh and blood.

The Bible in Psalms 37:37 tells us to "mark" the "perfect" man. The word *mark* means to "keep watch" and the word *perfect* means "whole or mature." What we are being told to do is keep our eyes on mature individuals, but not to idolize or make them a standard. If they are endeavoring to do things right based on the Word of God, simply follow their example.

Paul said, "Follow me as I follow Christ," which means we should follow only to the degree that if we were to step over to the side to see ahead of Paul, Christ would be in full view. We cannot walk blindly behind any individual, because when we do, we set ourselves up for failure.

I like to think of what Paul said this way. When I was a child, there were a lot of kids on our block. Every summer there was an ice cream truck that came down our street, and as soon as a child heard it coming, he would go from house to house screaming through windows or doors, "The ice cream truck is coming! The ice cream truck is coming!" We would run to our parents for money and quickly dash out the door behind our friend, who was following the truck. We were following the truck "as" our friend followed the truck. Our friend wasn't the one we were following; we were after the truck, but he was out there first and was encouraging us to follow along. So we joined him and we all ran together. That's what it means to "Follow me as I follow Christ." Paul wasn't telling them to follow him. He was saying, "I'm following Christ so let's go after Him together."

Paul was showing us that Christ, not another individual, is to be our focus. Our identity is in Him, and we are to be like Him. He is the standard by which we measure our lives. Follow after Him and He will take you places that your mind could never fathom.

God bless you!

Today's Scripture: Psalms 37:37.

Today's Prayer/Confession: I'm following Christ and I will lead others into a personal relationship with Him.

Obedience Is Essential

And these are God's instructions: "Gather enough for each person, about two quarts per person; gather enough for everyone in your tent." The People of Israel went to work and started gathering, some more, some less, but when they measured out what they had gathered, those who gathered more had no extra and those who gathered less weren't short—each person had gathered as much as was needed. Moses said to them, "Don't leave any of it until morning." But they didn't listen to Moses. A few of the men kept back some of it until morning. It got wormy and smelled bad. And Moses lost his temper with them. (Exodus 16:16–20 Message)

In Exodus 16, God told Moses that He would send manna from heaven every day to feed the children of Israel. They were not to take more than they needed, but just enough for their daily household. The only exception was the sixth day. On the sixth day, they were permitted to bring in double the amount in order to have enough for the Sabbath. Some failed to obey what God said and gathered extra, trying to store it for the next day. When they woke up the next morning, the leftover manna was rotted with worms and stunk.

That is what happens when we fail to obey God. The children of Israel didn't know that yesterday's manna wouldn't have the substance needed to fulfill them today. But God knew, and that was the reason He told them to take only what was needed for that day. Obedience is essential.

In order to move into the places that God has for us, we must learn to follow His instructions to the letter. The children of Israel gathered more than was necessary because they had a poverty mentality. Having done it before, they thought they would at some time go without food again. They wanted to make sure they had enough to avoid being hungry. God told them He would provide quail and manna for them every day, but they didn't trust Him—their disobedience proved it.

Obeying God is an outward manifestation of inward trust and dependency on God. Show Him that you trust Him by doing what you have been told, even if it doesn't make sense. In actuality it's not supposed to make sense, because it is a walk of faith. When you walk in obedience, you leave the realm of the senses, and by faith place your absolute confidence in God and His Word.

Obey what God says and His provision will be yours. Have a wonderful day!

Today's Scripture: Exodus 16:16–20.

Today's Prayer/Confession: I trust God with my whole heart. I trust Him enough to obey His instructions for my life. Today I will obey the voice of God, and I know I will prosper in all I do!

The Course of Life

Sometimes the hardest life to bring into subjection is your own. If you are a parent, you are acquainted with the constant duty of teaching your children to submit and obey. If you are an employer, you understand the need, as well as the challenges, of keeping employees in compliance. And although these may seem difficult, they don't come close to the challenges we can face when endeavoring to keep our own lives in line with God's established purpose.

*"The steps of a good man are **ordered** by the LORD: and he delighteth in his way"* (Psalms 37:23). As a believer, your life has already been mapped out by God—predetermined by Him. The word *ordered* in Psalms 37:23 means "prepared and secured." In other words, your path in life is a prepared and secure one, and everything you will ever need to walk it out is already firmly fixed. However, if we don't intentionally focus on keeping ourselves on that predetermined path, we can alter our course in life.

Challenges come against us on our spiritual journey just as they do on a natural journey. If we take a road trip, we can find ourselves dealing with the **elements, hindrances in the road, and distracting temptations**.

The elements represent unfavorable weather conditions. In the natural, various storms have brought complete devastation to cities and countries, ultimately causing people to abort their journeys.

The same is true when the storms of life "touch down" in our lives and we allow them to devastate our course. In Luke 8, we read the account of the disciples in the middle of a storm. Jesus had instructed them to go to the other side of the lake. Their course was predetermined, but the storm rose, threatening to destroy the boat and all within it. But Jesus came walking on the water and commanded them not to be afraid because He was with them. They were not allowed to abort their course, and they made it to the other side. The same holds true for you and me. The storms of life are coming, but we have to strap in, remember that Jesus is with us, and stay on course.

Hindrances in the road represent things like nails, glass, detours, and obstructions that slow down the journey. How many times have you been on the road and seen people stranded because of tire problems? Or have you ever been traveling on one road only to discover that a section is under construction and you have to detour for a period of time? The same holds true on our spiritual journey. There will be hindrances and some detours, but we have to stay on course. We have a real enemy, and he will throw whatever he can in the road to cause the "tires" of our lives to blow out. But in spite of his tactics, we quickly pull out our "spare," which is the Word of God, and keep moving.

When we sit on the side of the road and gripe and complain about how bad things are, Satan gets an advantage over us. He not only slows down our progress, but he also keeps us in a part of the journey longer than we should be there. But we are not ignorant of his devices (2 Corinthians 2:11). Through the Word of God we have the tools to keep things rolling in our lives.

With all that said, nothing thwarts the path of Christians like **distracting temptations**. Distracting temptations represent three things: the lust of the flesh, the lust of the eyes, and the pride of life (1 John 2:16). In the natural, my family and I have been on road trips where many times we have passed adult entertainment signs designed to draw people off the road and into their little hideaways. They are always conveniently located right off of the exit ramps. And unfortunately, everyone traveling the road sees the signs.

This very thing happens on our spiritual journey. Nothing on earth slows down or stops individuals from following God's plan like the lust of the flesh, the lust of the eyes, and the pride of life. They are like billboards or bright neon signs designed to pull you off course. They wait for their opportunity to find someone weak enough to fall into their clutches (Proverbs 7:7–27), and believe me, many have. To avoid being lured away, you will have to safeguard your eyes. This means putting the pedal to the metal by saying "no" to your fleshly desires, keeping your eyes away from sinful things and fixed on the pure things of God. It also means humbling yourself enough to recognize that no matter how long you may have been a Christian, the risk of getting off course is a reality for you if you don't guard your heart, ears and eyes.

Stay in God's face. Keep your life accountable to His Word, and you'll get through the course of life God has mapped out for you like a champion driver.

God bless you today!

Today's Scriptures: Psalms 37:23; Luke 8; 2 Corinthians 2:11; 1 John 2:16; Proverbs 7:7–27.

Today's Prayer/Confession: I will keep my eyes firmly fixed on the

Word of God and my ear finely tuned to the voice of God, following the course He has set out for my life. I will not stop, I will not quit, and I will not be hindered! I will not only run this race hard, but I will finish it well!

Discipline: The Path That Leads to Life

I want a healthier body ... discipline.
I want to spend more time with God ... discipline.
I want my bank account full ... discipline.
I want my way of thinking to change ... discipline.
I want to be consistent in relationships ... discipline.
I want to spend more time with my family ... discipline.
I want to be promoted in life ... discipline.

A disciplined lifestyle is more than just a great idea, it's the only way we will ever achieve all God has designed for us. Discipline takes time, fortitude, and stamina, and without it, our reach in life will fall short. Job 36:10 says that God opens ears to discipline. Have your ears been opened to hear?

Discipline has a voice that speaks to us every day of our lives. That's the voice that tells us to get up and pray, even when we don't feel like it. His voice is the one that says "That's enough!" when we want more and "Don't do it!" when everything in us wants to do it anyway.

Discipline is the hand of God heavy upon us, guiding us down the path of life (Psalms 32:4 NLT). Although it may be rough, discipline is our friend. Isaiah said it leads to health and life (Isaiah 38:16). Solomon said it purifies the heart (Proverbs 20:30). And David said happiness comes to those who submit to it (Psalms 94:12).

Several years ago, my twin brother competed for the Olympics as a weightlifter. Because I was impressed with his physique, I decided that I would give weightlifting a try. I didn't realize all that went into shaping and sculpting the body. I walked in the door and watched him work out—and walked out the door and never went back. I wasn't prepared mentally to undergo that type of discipline, so I decided that body building wasn't for me.

That's the way it is with many of us. We can see God causing other people to prosper, and we may want what they have, but when the rubber meets the road, we decide it's not for us because we don't want to go through the things that other people are willing to go through. You have to be willing to endure something in order to have what you desire. Nothing comes to us in life without a price, and the price that we have been called to pay is the price of discipline.

Hebrews 12:11 in the New Living Translation says: "*No discipline is enjoyable while it is happening, it is painful! But afterward there will be a quiet harvest of right living for those who are trained in this way.*" Let discipline be your friend. In the end, you'll be all that God has destined you to be! Have a great day!

Today's Scriptures: Job 36:10; Psalms 32:4; Isaiah 38:16; Proverbs 20:30; Psalms 94:12; Hebrews 12:11.

Today's Prayer/Confession: I will submit to the hand of discipline, and every day I will obey the voice of the Holy Spirit as He leads and guides me down the path of life.